"Dr. Benesh is helping lead the way in urban church planting. This is a must-read for those considering the future of church planting in a multi-nucleated urban context. The walkable church is here. Let Sean's word in this book serve as your personal Urban City Guide."

Wes Hughes
Urban Church Planting Catalyst
Portland, Oregon

"Sean Benesh is a practitioner who is also doing theological work—and in the fastest growing, most complex human environments in our world. Moreover, he loves the city and understands the nuance of place. His analysis contributes to a more effective and incarnational engagement for the church. Thanks Sean!"

Leonard Hjalmarson
Adjunct Professor of Ministry at Northern Baptist Theological Seminary, Chicago and co-author of *Missional Spirituality* and *No Home Like Place*

"Without question our future is an urban future and all of life will be impacted as a result. For years urban missiologists have been telling us that our church planting methodology will need to adapt to the urban environment, but few have ventured forward with ideas about how to go about doing this. In this book, Sean Benesh has done just this. He brings a cogent understanding of cities together with a passion for vibrant churches to be started in cities."

Michael Crane
Director of Institute of Urban Studies in Asia

"Sean Benesh points out the logic of strategizing church planting efforts around public transportation networks in the multi-nucleated urban environment. On the neighborhood level he demonstrates the importance of pedestrian-oriented design in enhancing connectivity, building community as well as diversity and equity. I commend Sean for studying contemporary urban design and having it impact the conversation about urban church planting."

Guy de Lijster
Transit / Urban Designer
Seattle, Washington

The Multi-Nucleated Church

Towards a Theoretical Framework for Church Planting in High-Density Cities

Sean Benesh

Foreword by Linda Bergquist

Urban Loft Publishers | Portland, Oregon

The Multi-Nucleated Church
Towards a Theoretical Framework for Church Planting in High-Density Cities

First published 2012
Second edition 2015

Copyright © 2015 Sean Benesh. All rights reserved. Except for brief quotations in critical publications or reviews, no part of this book may be reproduced in any manner without prior written permission from the publisher. Write: Permissions, Urban Loft Publishers, 2034 NE 40th Avenue, #414, Portland, OR 97212.

Urban Loft Publishers
2034 NE 40th Avenue #414
Portland, OR 97212
www.theurbanloft.org

ISBN-13: 978-0692360774
ISBN-10:0692360778

Manufactured in the U.S.A

Unless otherwise indicated, all Scripture quotations are from The Holy Bible, English Standard Version® (ESV®), copyright © 2001 by Crossway, a publishing ministry of Good News Publishers. Used by permission. All rights reserved.

Contents

About the Metrospiritual Book Series // 7
Foreword by Linda Bergquist // 9
Preface to the Second Edition // 15
Preface // 19
Acknowledgements // 23
Introduction // 25

1 Framework:
   Multi-Nucleated and High-Density (*The System*) // 29
2 Living and Planting in a Multi-Nucleated City // 41
3 Foundation:
   Walkable and Pedestrian-Scale (*The Hub*) // 59
4 Life in Dense Urban Settings // 69
5 Church Planting in Multi-Nucleated Hubs // 87
6 Function:
   Transportation-Centered Ecclesiology (*The Spokes*) // 101
7 Multi-Nucleated Ecclesiology // 113

   Afterword // 127
   Bibliography // 131
   About Urban Loft Publishers // 135
   Author // 136
   Books in the Metrospiritual Book Series // 137

To those who are embodying the Kingdom on foot and by bike.

Metrospiritual Books Series

In my first book, *Metrospiritual*, I was looking for a term, as well as a way, to define what an urban-centric approach to faith and Scripture looked like. This came about as I wrestled through how do we reconcile the urban trajectory of humanity throughout Scripture, the current state of rapid urbanization and globalization, along with where we'll spend eternity. In a similar tone, with the church still applying a rural or suburban lens in which to view life, faith, and Scripture, it is time for a new set of lenses. This is what I call metrospiritual. I define it as this, "It is taking an urban lens to the reading, understanding, interpretation, and application of Scripture." The Metrospiritual Book Series explores various aspects, elements, ideas, methodologies, and theology of what an urban-centric faith looks like expressed in the city. A metrospirituality can have a shaping effect on the way the church lives in, loves, serves, embraces, and engages the city with the Good News of the Kingdom of God.

Sean Benesh

Foreword

Like Sean Benesh, I am a lover of large, intense, pulsating cities. When my family travels, we visit New York, Delhi, Mexico City, and Tokyo. My personal fear factor rises in the country and subsides in these, the world's most populous cities. In 1996 I moved to San Francisco as a church planter strategist. The assumption was that since I had been effectively mobilizing church planting in San Diego for over a decade, I would be able to do the same thing in other cities too. For years, almost everything I did failed, mostly because I really did not understand the difference between a sprawling suburban city and a dense urban center.

In those days, it did not occur to me that I needed an interpreter to help me analyze and understand my city. That I loved her was not enough. While I had married her, for better or for worse, I needed to read her pulse—to know what made her tick and to understand what an indigenous expression of the bride of Christ could look like there. However, no interpreters were to be found in those days, and few are

The Multi-Nucleated Church

available to the church even now. While there are many things I appreciate about this book, what I like most about it is that it helps to fill that particular knowledge gap and lets me know that I am not alone in my quest.

This is such an opportune time for the release of this book for the church planting world, and for this I am grateful. As of January 1, 2012, there were 481 cities in the world with populations of a million or more. Twenty-seven of these have populations of over 10 million. China is in the process of combining several cities in a region to create a mega city of 42 million residents. With this rapid rise in the urban population, we must learn to better understand how real cities work, or our church planting / evangelistic efforts simply won't touch their lostness.

In previous decades, many of us interpreted our church planting callings in light of a skewed interpretation of the church of the church growth movement. We assumed that to "go where God was moving" meant to choose church fields where numerical growth was the most immediately productive. It meant finding those new, sprawling housing communities where there were most certainly already Christians who needed a local church. In those kinds of places, certainly church could be franchised, since their relative homogeneity allowed for a "one-style-fits-all" approach. Church planting still flourishes in these kinds of places, and certainly this is needed.

Foreword

Today, however, a Kingdom mentality has supplanted the church growth mindset. Instead of seeking out communities that almost guarantee the potential for large successful churches, the best planters are asking questions like, "Which are the greatest pockets of darkness that most need an infusion of Christ's light?" Newly in love with cities, they are moving to the urban core. My fear is that many will give up too soon, because they bring with them rules of engagement designed for suburbs.

Some of the concepts in this book are brand new to me, even though I have studied cities for many years. For example, I had never heard of the concept of a multi-nucleated city, where there are multiple business/residential hubs in one city rather than a single central business district (CBD). The concept makes sense to me. San Francisco's new, upscale Mission Bay neighborhood is a city within a city. It houses thousands of new residences, is home to three new hospitals, many new tech industries, genetic research organizations, non-profits, and restaurants. Most people who live there do not even own a car, and even those who come in from the outside to work use various forms of public transportation. Mission Bay is the new kind of urban-chic city written with an alternative value system as presented in this book. San Francisco's working Chinatown is not urban chic, but it is another kind of all-in-one community. Generations of Chinese who live in this neighborhood need never leave there to work at their shops, eat noodles, play mahjong, or worship at the Buddhist temple. Automobiles belong to tourists, not residents.

I do understand Sean's practical "theology of transportation" and its implications for church planting. Recently San Francisco's Board of Supervisors voted that commercial building owners can allow employees to bring their bicycles indoors while they are working. The city experienced a 71 percent increase in bike ridership in just five years and has a goal that 20 percent of all vehicle trips in the city be by bike by 2020. When people walk, bike, or use public transportation to get to and from work, how will they choose to attend worship services? How does that affect Sunday church attendance when public transportation systems operate less regularly on Sundays? Which of our church buildings house indoor bike lots?

The concept of a multi-nucleated church also carries with it incredible possibilities for movement. Structurally, movements are decentralized, interconnected and segmented (meaning that they look differently in different places). A church for Chinatown, for example, looks different than a church in Mission Bay, downtown, or one of the city's other CBDs. They are naturally decentralized, partly because the city is, and they are connected to one another around mission, such as in the church studies presented in this book. These things are not movement makers, but they serve as runners along which movements thrive.

If we love our cities, we will care enough to romance them by listening to them and by seeking to understand them. Sean Benesh is a city lover full of wise counsel that can help you love your city too.

Linda Bergquist
Church Planting Catalyst, San Francisco
Author of *The Wholehearted Church Planter* and *Church Turned Inside Out*

The Multi-Nucleated Church

Preface to the Second Edition

The ability to access data and information occurs with a rapidity unparalleled in our human existence. The turnaround time on research is instantaneous and we have the ability to immediately dispense this to the mass population. It is not an overstatement to say that the internet continues to transform our lives. In terms of this book what I specifically have in mind are the repercussions this is having on the publishing world.

Earlier in the year I and two colleagues who are both professors of urban ministry in their respective schools were in conversations with several publishing companies about the need for a book updating the whole issue of urban ministry in the twenty-first century. One publisher in particular was very interested ... but there was a catch. They wanted to publish the book *five years from now*. In today's world five years is an eternity given how rapidly our world is changing and the new information we continue to uncover.

The book you hold in your hands got its start while I sat in a coffee shop in Portland, Oregon, in the fall of 2011. By the spring of 2012 the book was finished and a few months later it was published. Now it's the late fall of 2014. That means three years have gone by since I first undertook this project. In three years it seems as though the world has changed once again. My outlook too has changed the more I've read and as I've conducted new research. I've experienced more, travelled more, and engaged in more conversations relevant to the topics in this book. All of this has in a way haunted me because it made me realize that this book needed not only to be updated but expanded as well.

While the framework and focus of this book is still the same in regards to planting churches in high-density cities around active transportation, much of what has changed is not only the new and expanded information it contains, but me as well. You see, while I have been involved in church planting as a planter and strategist since 2003 my role continues to change. More specifically, I am no longer a church planter (which I have to admit I was not very good at). Instead my role has shifted to working with church planters across North America in the capacity of training and facilitating conversations about what it means to plant churches in the city of the twenty-first century.

Since I am no longer a church planter, for this second edition I have intentionally changed the language. That is to say, the *voice* is of one who now works with church planters through education and research rather me trying to plant multiplying churches. I hope this will be a helpful update on how we can redefine and re-imagine planting the Gospel by means of new churches in today's growing high-density cities.

The Multi-Nucleated Church

Preface

This book has its genesis in Vancouver, British Columbia, Canada. It was while living in this high-density polycentric city that the concept of a theoretical framework for a multi-nucleated church began to take shape. Fast forward to our new home in Portland, Oregon, south of the Canadian border but still in the Pacific Northwest. This tale of two rather unique cities in two different countries provides the backdrop against which these concepts are hammered out. Each city, with its own unique built environment[1] and urbanism,[2] molds and shapes what the multi-nucleated church looks like … or *can look like*.

---

[1] The "built environment" of a city refers to the human-made or artificial surroundings and setting upon which human activity is carried out. This encompasses such things as buildings, the transportation infrastructure, and anything else human-made. Far from being simply mechanistic in nature, the built environment can also be viewed as an organism.

[2] "Urbanism" is broadly defined here as the culture or way of life of city dwellers. Some definitions entail the overall vibe or characteristics of cities which includes the built environment.

In church planting circles we are more apt to look backwards rather than forwards when talking about models, methods, forms, and expressions. This concept of reverse-engineering is the topic of many books on church planting as leaders reflect on what worked, and what worked wildly well. To propose a theoretical framework is to take the reverse approach, a forward trajectory. Also, to float ideas, concepts, and a way of church planting not predicated on the luxury of reverse-engineering is counter-intuitive, yet normative in society as a whole. It is akin to an architect conceptualizing, drawing, and then creating a 3D model of what is yet to come. The architect takes into account the prevalent dynamics prior to the conceptualizing and building phase. Context begins to determine the framework for what the architect has to work with. For example, he or she would need to know if this the client has a new building in mind, or is reclaiming an old historic building in a downtown district.

This is what I aim to do with this book, namely to show the importance of context in determining the framework for what the church planter has to work with. Its subtitle clarifies my intentions: *Towards a Theoretical Framework for Church Planting in High-Density Cities*. It is my desire and motivation to elevate church planting in high-density cities and contexts. Portland certainly is not considered high-density compared to numerous other cities, but there are districts and

Preface

neighborhoods that are certainly higher in density, and where it becomes normative to live life on the pedestrian scale.

The catalyst behind writing this book was a paper on the topic of church planting in polycentric cities that Michael Crane, a seminary professor in Southeast Asia, asked me to submit for a class he was teaching. Knowing some of the dynamics of this context, having lived in Vancouver and now Portland, that paper widened the scope of my appreciation for the need to explore church planting in such cities as these. For too long church planting literature and training has been primarily focused on starting churches in low-density parts of our cities, predicated upon auto-based commuting patterns. However, the reality of the global city is that millions upon millions of people worldwide do not live that kind of lifestyle. Rather, life for them revolves around getting from Point A to Point B whether it be on foot, or via a bicycle or public transportation. What would church planting look like in the context of such common transportation realities? Instead of basing strategies and methodologies on a car-based lifestyle, *The Multi-Nucleated Church* reduces the scale to walkable neighborhoods, districts, and central cities. The common denominator is the truly high-density urban context. This book seeks to advance that conversation.

The Multi-Nucleated Church

Acknowledgements

There are a few people that I would like to thank and acknowledge who helped in different ways in this project. Special thanks to one of my students, Danielle McDade, for looking over the manuscript and copyediting the first edition. More than simply correcting my grammatical mistakes, she helped create a better flow to the book. Many thanks!!! Thanks to Caleb Crider and Wes Hughes for all of those Thursday morning coffee gatherings at Ristretto Roasters on North Williams where we talked all-things Portland, church planting, and dreamed together about training the next generation of church planters and urban thinkers. While as a result of job relocation we're not able to meet any longer, our conversations helped stimulate some of the ideas in this book.

I am appreciative of Michael Crane who asked me to submit a paper about church planting in multi-nucleated cities which evolved into this book. I also appreciated his feedback and input on the manuscript. Thanks to Len Hjalmarson who gave me invaluable insight and feedback on some key concepts in this book. Thanks to my friend Frank Stirk whose copyedited a good number of my books and has done so again on this second edition.

Introduction

The more I delve into the study of cities from various angles and perspectives, the more I am seeing a clear delineation in what people deem "urban ministry." Oftentimes books, articles, or journals labeled "urban ministry" usually fall into classic demarcations of what urban life is ... or *was*. Here is what the equation looked like when I was growing up:

Inner-city = Bad, unsafe, unsavory, full of crime, gangs, violence, racial tensions, degraded buildings, blight.

Suburbs = White, safe, homogeneous, sterile, sprawling, big grassy lawns, morally and politically conservative.

Of course not every city looked like that; nor was this the case everywhere. But the central premise is clear. Most urban ministry books written about this era (and still today) detailed the work among low-income ethnic families, creating economic vitality, improving public schools, racial reconciliation, inducing suburbanites to move back into the city to counter white flight, and a life of risk and adventure which was not for the faint of heart. Indeed there are many places today that still share those characteristics. However, urban ministry has changed and continues to change right before our eyes, not simply in North America, but globally as well. For example, around the time I graduated from high school in 1992, the Pudong in Shanghai was full of rice fields. Now the density of the built environment of the Pudong is a global postcard-worthy icon. This is what the equation more and more is looking like, particularly in North America (even though gentrification and urban revitalization comprise truly a global movement):

> *Inner-city* = Cool, hip, full of hipsters, singlespeed bikes, cafes, micro-breweries, art galleries, revitalized economic outlook, reclaimed historic buildings, expensive, desirable, politically, sexually, and morally liberal.
>
> *Suburbs* = Changing, inner-ring suburbs are becoming the landing place for the displaced urban poor, still low-density although many are attempting to retro-fit suburbia with higher-density clusters mixed with light rail, still looked down upon for their blatant sterility, and still conservative (although that's changing).

Again, these are generic observations or characteristics that fit some cities better than others. But what this reveals is the changing landscape of the urban frontier … in fact there's a *new* urban frontier. Urban is now associated with elite, sophisticated, educated, and hip. Suburban is becoming the catch-basin for the migrating urban poor. Here is what this brings to the forefront ... we need a new era of authors researching and writing under the rubric of the new urban frontier. For that I hope to be one voice among many.

The new urban frontier is a recalibration of the former way of urban life which means the old labels do not always apply (e.g., inner-city = bad). We need researchers and authors under the banner of urban ministry who will write about ministry to the suburban poor. We also need more research into the changing urban fabric brought on by dense globalization and the burgeoning creative or knowledge-based economy. My hope is that this short book can help move this conversation forward and be part of the researching, writing, thinking, and conversations taking place about what this "new" kind of ministry ought to look like as we head deeper into the twenty-first century.

We need to embrace this new urban reality ... the *new urban frontier.*

The Multi-Nucleated Church

Chapter 1

Framework: Multi-Nucleated and High-Density (The System)

The city is not a static entity. Since its inception, the city has been in flux, adapting, changing, and evolving more like an organism than some mechanical contraption. As the pace of urbanization, especially in developing nations,[1] continues to pick up exponentially, it has caused a reorienting phenomenon for global citizens. Jeb Brugmann aptly states, "The media have been keen to report that 'half the world's population now live in cities,' but we are overlooking the main event: half the world has become *the City*."[2] The world is now urban. Not only is humanity en masse migrating to the city, but this has caused,

---

[1] "A total of 193,107 new city dwellers are added to the world's urban population daily. This translates to 5 million new urban dwellers per month in the developing world and 500,000 in developed countries." UN-HABITAT, *Global Report on Human Settlement 2009*, 26.

[2] Brugmann, *Welcome to the Urban Revolution*, 10.

in some cases, the city's built environment to be reflective of this burgeoning population. "Future urban planning must take place within an understanding of the factors shaping 21st-century cities, especially the demographic, environmental, economic and socio-spatial challenges that lie ahead. It also needs to recognize the changing institutional structure of cities and the emerging spatial configuration of large, multiple-nuclei or polycentric, city-regions."[3] It is to this topic of the built environment of the city, in particular the multi-nucleated or polycentric[4] form of urban planning, that forms the foundation for exploring what church planting looks like in these contexts. The result of this reconfiguration is what I have called the *multi-nucleated church*.

I was first exposed to this concept of while preparing for our move to Vancouver. We felt prompted by the Lord to move to this cosmopolitan world-class city to begin church planting. Simultaneously, I was finishing up my dissertation which became *Metrospiritual: The Geography of Church Planting*, where I initially began to write about church planting in the context of a multi-nucleated city. Part of my doctoral process exposed me to some of the basic tenets of urban geography. I studied the development of cities, from their dusty origins in the ancient Near East, all of the way up to the current aberrations in various North American cities, as

---

[3] *Global Report on Human Settlement 2009*, xxii.

[4] From here forward I will use *multi-nucleated* and *polycentric* interchangeably.

Chapter 1

well as spending time in Shanghai and Beijing, China. One thing that became abundantly clear is how cities are shaped and formed revolves around something seemingly benign ... transportation technologies.

Edward Glaeser asserts, "Transportation technologies have always determined urban form."[5] I use that quote a lot. Earlier this week I cited it as I walked the streets of Basse-Ville (Lower Town) in Quebec City with a group of church leaders. The allure of these attractive neighborhoods with their seventeenth-century streetscape can be tied directly to the fact that this part of the city was built when the primary mode of transportation was by foot. As a result the streets are narrow and the buildings are compact. This stands in stark contrast to life on the suburban periphery of this same city which was built for the automobile with its strip malls and single-family homes with expansive yards. The only way to manage daily life is to drive.

Authors Peter Newman, Timothy Beatley, and Heather Boyer trace the development of these transportation technologies and their ensuing effect on the urban built environment.

> *Walking Cities* were (and are) dense, mixed-use areas of no more than five kilometers across. These were the major urban form for eight thousand years and in substantial parts of cities like Ho Chi Minh, Mumbai, and Hong

---

[5] Glaeser, *Triumph of the City*, 12.

Kong, the character of a walking city has been retained. Krakow is mostly a walking city. In wealthy cities like New York, San Francisco, Chicago, London, Vancouver, and Sydney, the central areas are mostly walking cities in character.

Transit Cities from 1850 to 1950 were based on trains and trams, which meant they could spread twenty to thirty kilometers with dense centers and corridors following rail lines and stations. Most European and wealthy Asian cities retain this form, and the old U.S., Australian, and Canadian inner cities are also transit oriented. Many developing cities in Asia, Africa, and Latin America have the dense corridors form of a transit city but don't always have the transit systems to support them; thus they become car-saturated.

Automobile Cities from the early 1950s on, could spread fifty to eighty kilometers in all directions and at low density. U.S., Canadian, Australian, and New Zealand and many new parts of European cities began to develop in this way, but these new areas are reaching the limits of a half hour car commute as they sprawl outward. These are the most vulnerable areas to the oil peak.[6]

Glaeser also highlights the differences brought on by changing transportation technologies:

In walking cities, like central Florence or Jerusalem's old city; the streets are narrow, winding, and crammed with shops. When people had to use their legs to get around, they tried to get as close as possible to each other and to the waterways that provided the fastest way into or out of

---

[6] Newman, et al, *Resilient Cities*, 89.

the city. Areas built around trains and elevators, like midtown Manhattan and the Chicago Loop, have wider streets often organized in a grid. There are still shops on the streets, but most of the office space is much further from the ground. Cities built around the car, like much of Los Angeles and Phoenix and Houston, have enormous gently curving roads and often lack sidewalks. In those places, shops and pedestrians retreat from the streets into malls. While older cities usually have an obvious center, dictated by an erstwhile port or a rail station, car cities do not. They just stretch toward the horizon in un-differentiated urban sprawl.[7]

From Monocentric to Polycentric Cities

The twentieth-century understanding of cities was dominated by Concentric Zone Model[8] of urban development, which followed the spatial layout of Chicago as an example or template. The basic theory, based on the development patterns of Chicago, was that there are distinct zones that radiate from the center beginning with the Central Business District (CBD). "University of Chicago sociologist Ernest W. Burgess pioneered the systematic study of the North American city's internal structure. In the 1920s, he developed a model of internal city structure and urban growth: the so-called Burgess concentric zone model or hypothesis. This model grew out of Burgess' fascination with Chicago, a

---

[7] *Triumph of the City*, 12-13.

[8] Created by sociologist Ernest Burgess in 1924.

remarkable city at a remarkable time."[9] The zones are listed as following:

- Central Business District
- Factory Zone
- Zone of Transition
- Working Class Zone
- Residential Zone
- Commuter Zone[10]

The Concentric Zone Model is also referred to as a Monocentric City. "The traditional structure of Western cities is Monocentric, with a high density commercial core surrounded by residential suburbs. This structure provides strong support for radial public transport journeys, but it tends to increase travel distances, and exacerbate congestion due to tidal commuting flows."[11] Many North American cities are reflective of this reality. The closer one gets to the city center and CBD the greater the density becomes. Few cities have taken an aggressive approach to urban planning to correct this. The Chicago School, as it was called, has become deeply imbedded in the urban fabric of many cities.

As the twentieth century wore on and was drawing to a close the Chicago School was being challenged by the Los

---

[9] Phillips, *City Lights*, 530.

[10] Ibid., 531.

[11] Smith, "Polycentric Cities and Sustainable Development."

Chapter 1

Angeles School. The contrast between these two schools of thought paves the way for our discussion of the polycentric city. "While the Chicago School presents a modernist theory of cities as based on social darwinist struggles for urban space, the Los Angeles School proposes a postmodern or postfordist vision."[12] One of the proponents and voices of the LA School, Michael Dear, contends that, "Los Angeles has become, for many, not the exception but rather a prototype of the city of the future."[13] In many ways, Vancouver shares a lot in common with Los Angeles as far as a dispersed polycentric city. However, what LA lacks Vancouver has: density.

The premise of a multi-nucleated city is the concept that, "High density mixed-use centres bring activities closer together and are thought to reduce travel distances, and so encourage more efficient walking and public transportation trips."[14] In other words, rather than one main central area with high density (the downtown core), polycentric cities seek to regulate traffic into the CBD by "dispersal" and "densification" which take place simultaneously. "It is worth noting that some of the CBD's symbolic sparkle means less and less to more and more U.S. metropolitanites these days. Why? Because with the shifts of people, jobs, cultural venues, and retail trade to U.S. suburban and posturban areas, fewer people need to go

---

[12] Wikimedia Foundation Inc., "Los Angeles School."

[13] Dear, *From Chicago to L.A.*, vii.

[14] "Polycentric Cities and Sustainable Development."

'downtown' for jobs, goods, services, or entertainment."[15] The notion of "dispersal" and "densification" has been the methodology adopted by Metro Vancouver and their Livable Region Strategic Plan. "What Metro Vancouver started and is in the process of fulfilling is to compact the population, jobs, and businesses into high-density clusters known as 'city centers' or 'municipal centers.' Dotted throughout the Metro area are these unique city centers that act as regional hubs for that part of the city."[16] Metro Vancouver's website goes to describe their concept of Livable Centres:

> In the Livable Region Strategic Plan, the foundation of the complete communities concept is the network of regional and municipal town centres. Municipal town centres serve a number of neighbourhoods and/or are the main centre for the smaller municipalities. They have a smaller catchment than the regional town centres. They are intended to provide business and community facilities, together with opportunities for medium and higher-density residential development in both ground-oriented housing and apartments. They would contain a mixture of municipal-serving businesses and local services, be transit and pedestrian-oriented, and generally be linked by bus connections to the regional transportation system. The Strategic Plan identifies 13 municipal town centres, although municipal plans may include others.[17]

---

[15] *City Lights*, 549.

[16] Benesh, *Metrospiritual*, 6.

[17] Metro Vancouver, "Livable Centres."

The four building blocks of this strategy are: protect the green zone, build complete communities, achieve a compact metropolitan region, and increase transportation choice.[18] One of the cities that make up the metro area, North Vancouver, which sits just across Burrard Inlet from Vancouver's downtown core, references the Livable Region Strategic Plan on its website. "It delineates a metropolitan core represented by the City of Vancouver, and eight inter-connected Regional Town Centres which are further complemented by smaller Municipal Town Centres."[19] Some of the strategies of this plan take shape accordingly:

>   *Goal 1*—Create a Compact Urban Area
>   *Strategy 1.1*—Contain urban development within the urban containment boundary.
>   *Strategy 1.2*—Focus growth in urban centres and frequent transit development corridors.
>   *Strategy 1.3*—Encourage land use and transportation developments that reduce greenhouse gas emissions.
>   *Strategy 1.4*—Protect rural lands.
>
>   *Goal 2*—Support a Sustainable Economy
>   *Strategy 2.1*—Promote a pattern of land development that supports diverse regional economy and employment close to where people live.
>   *Strategy 2.2*—Protect the region's supply of industrial land.

---

[18] White, "Draft Metro Vancouver Regional Growth Strategy," 9.

[19] The City of North Vancouver, "Livable Region Strategic Plan."

Goal 3—Protect the Region's Natural Areas

Goal 4—Develop Complete and Resilient Communities
Strategy 4.1—Provide diverse and affordable housing options.
Strategy 4.2—Develop complete, inclusive communities with access to a range of services.

Goal 5—Support Sustainable Transportation Choices
Strategy 5.1—Connect land use and transportation to support transit, walking, and cycling.
Strategy 5.2—Connect land use and transportation to support an efficient roads and goods movement network.[20]

This concept of creating compact cities leverages *proximity* and *density* which can be called *urban advantage*. "The further concentration of hundreds of millions in cities, whether through risk-taking squatter communities, multinational companies, ethnic groups, social movements, guerrilla movements, or transnational gangs, reflects the multitude of strategies to claim some bit of control over a city's urban advantage so they can leverage it *for their own advantage*. If we don't understand what makes up urban advantage, then we can't understand the City."[21]

Glaeser picks up on this insight: "Cities grow by building up, or out, and when a city doesn't build, people are prevented

---

[20] "Draft Metro Vancouver Regional Growth Strategy," 5-7.

[21] *Welcome to the Urban Revolution*, 24.

from experiencing the magic of urban proximity."[22] This is the direction that Metro Vancouver is moving towards. Not only does creating a multi-nucleated or polycentric city make sense economically and foster more sustainable transportation, it also unleashes the potential and benefit that proximity creates. "Urban density creates a constant flow of new information that comes from observing others' successes and failures."[23] Lastly, densification seems to be the urban trajectory for the future. "Urbanization and higher-density living is an irreversible path of human development."[24]

So what does it then look like to plant churches in polycentric or multi-nucleated cities?

---

[22] *Triumph of the City*, 136.

[23] Ibid., 247.

[24] Ng, *Designing High-Density Cities*, xxxi.

The Multi-Nucleated Church

Chapter 2

Living and Planting in a Multi-Nucleated City

While in Metro Vancouver, my family and I lived in Edmonds Town Centre, which was one of four of such town centers in the city of Burnaby. Through life in this city center, that was interconnected to the rest of the Metro area by Skytrain, buses, and bike paths, we learned that we could function well without the need of a car. The density of the city centers, which held all of the amenities we needed, plus a ubiquitous transit system that connected us to the other city centers, made life not only enjoyable, but began forming the foundation for church planting in these multi-nucleated cities.

When it comes to church planting in the city, and in multi-nucleated cities in particular, any strategy or methodology needs to be adapted to the current context of the city which most certainly includes the built environment. In *Metrospiritual* I noted, "The shaping forces of cities play an enormous role in the geography of church planting. The decision of where to start a church in a metropolitan area is critical to the future trajectory of the church because the setting or context influences so much."[1] The goal for me was to design church planting around the city's urban form. This involves adapting basic forms and models of the way the church looked in the New Testament to accommodate the polycentric mega-global city. Along with that is the need to uncover or explore the theological implications of the built environment of our cities.

Canadian professor William McAlpine writes, "I would argue that the built environment, and in particular sacred spaces associated with and produced by culture, provides one of the most significant windows into understanding that culture."[2] When we start with a theological framework for our city it leads towards a specific response. "A theology of the built environment is more than merely an academic discipline. The end goal is not only for us to understand our cities, but to begin seeing them through a theological lens. That in turn leads us into exploring our cities further, and ultimately to love them and see them the way God does. And that can lead to only one response: taking action."[3] Rather than creating church planting strategies and methodologies for how

---

[1] Benesh, *Metrospiritual*, 117.

[2] McAlpine, *Sacred Space for the Missional Church*, 13.

[3] Benesh, *View From the Urban Loft*, 150.

churches should function, it would be more impactful to let the built form of cities guide and lead in this regard, but doing so with a theological lens.

Eric Jacobsen notes, "We've given very little thought to the physical structure of our cities and how that provides the framework for the human relationships that go on in these places."[4] As an extreme example, we admit that we would go about church planting differently if we were on the Steppes of Mongolia compared to the canyon-like high-rise residential towers of Hong Kong. The physicality of space dictates *how* we do church planting. Again, the foundation of church planting was laid in the New Testament so this is not a deviation from first-century principles, but instead an attempt to adapt them to current urban form.

One of the lectures that I now have given on numerous occasions is called "Urban Form, Missiology, and Church Planting." The premise is to discuss and explore how urban form influences, or at least *ought* to influence, the *how* of church planting. To illustrate my point I present numerous slides featuring images from different cities around the world. I use such images as sprawling suburbia in Phoenix to a mass of cyclists in Amsterdam to compact residential towers in Tokyo. For each photo we address the following question: How does the built environment of this part of the city

---

[4] Jacobsen, *Sidewalks in the Kingdom*, 65.

influence (or should influence) the way that we go about church planting?

Too often in church planting it is easy to neglect the overall urbanism of one's host city as an overall influential factor as to how church is done and expressed. I contend that the "cultural soil dictates much of how churches are being planted, or at least it should."[5] The idea behind planting churches this way is not to be creative or innovative. Rather, it is to apply a theological and missiological lens or framework for understanding context and adapting strategies accordingly. This opens the door to further discussion in the areas of cultivating a theology of place or theology of the built environment. "Constructing a theology of place must consider the context of where the *missio Dei* is to take place."[6] Or as Hirsch and Catchm put it, "A model's success is always dependent on a certain level of congruence between that model and its environment."[7]

From here forward I aim to develop this strategy towards a theoretical framework for planting in these types of contexts, conceptualizing a multi-nucleated church for a multi-nucleated city. There are few models currently attempting this. However, that does not mean there are not more out there. Notable exceptions are some multi-site churches that have bits

---

[5] *Metrospiritual*, 119.

[6] *View From the Urban Loft*, 135.

[7] Hirsch and Catchim, *The Permanent Revolution*, xxxiv.

and pieces of this framework in their strategy, whether intentionally or not.[8] The difference lies in designing strategy around urban form and transportation technologies. With that said, I will present the working framework for church planting in these settings that was influenced by my living both in Vancouver and Portland. From the very beginning Vancouver's urbanism crept into the core values of our church planting efforts. Out of the several core values that I began developing to guide our church planting efforts, one was related solely to transportation. Not simply transportation in general, but more specifically about walkability or active transportation as a guiding value. So why walkability? It seemed from the outset that this is antithetical to the way most churches develop and grow.

The result of focusing on the pedestrian-scale and walkability is that it elevates the chance for investment in the local neighborhood that otherwise might be missing if the church is built and grows based upon the auto-based commuter mentality. In the middle of church planting I wrote:

> Maybe this is truly a purist movement and nonsensical, but when it comes to the Ion Community [our church planting attempt], the goal is to reverse that trend by putting worshipping communities in the city centers. That

---

[8] Some interesting work on the ecclesiological side can be found in Hirsch and Catchim, *The Permanent Revolution.* A post-denominational expression of a local and apostolic network would fit beautifully in a multi-nucleated context.

it makes it accessible to those who want to simply walk or bike. My hope is that this elevates the love, care, and investment in the immediate neighborhood and city center. This is what makes Ion walkable. With the focus being on a walkable church, it also ties into the idea of being an interconnected network that utilizes the existing transit system to plant churches and stay connected.[9]

Later in this book I will lay out a more detailed framework for church planting in these city centers, predicated upon the concept of pedestrian-oriented church planting and walkable churches. Then we will look at how churches in these hubs or city centers can be interconnected with one another through the various transportation options available.

To summarize, I am advocating that: (1) urban form dictates the *how* of church planting (while being guided by New Testament principles), (2) a new approach to church planting in multi-nucleated (and high-density) cities needs to develop around transportation technologies, (3) church planting networks in these settings can be both "dense" and "dispersed" as they are rooted in city centers but interconnected with other churches in the other city centers, and (4) the foundation of community in the church life of a city center needs to be pedestrian-oriented or walkable (and bike-friendly) which makes it accessible for those who live in such places. This was what we were attempting to build in Vancouver. Since there were several circumstances which

---

[9] *Metrospiritual*, 157.

prompted us to relocate back to the United States after only two years, we were not able to see this come to fruition. We left no church behind in the city other than two campus ministries that we had started in two city centers. With that said, I will share what church planting in a multi-nucleated city looked like and what took place during our time in Vancouver.

Leading up to relocating to Vancouver, through an urban geography course I was taking, I was exposed to this concept of a polycentric city, and for additional reading I chose to delve further into Vancouver's story. I learned how the city was plotted out and the progression through various transportation technologies which shaped the city ranging from streetcars of yesteryear to the Skytrain of today. I was acquainted with the city center concept which began finding its way into our church planting strategy and basic church ecclesiology. I sought to embrace what authors Eric Swanson and Sam Williams noted in *To Transform a City:* "Becoming an expert on your city also comes about through an 'exegesis' of your city."[10]

---

[10] Swanson and Williams, *To Transform a City*, 168.

The Struggle of Church Planting in a Multi-Nucleated City

Upon arrival in Vancouver we spent the first two weeks looking for a place to live. Our basic criterion was to be located in a dense city center so we would have a walkable neighborhood with a variety of transportation options. We found a place to live in Edmonds Town Centre, where we had access to designated bike paths that took me into the downtown core and other city centers, a Skytrain station, and ample bus stops for routes that would deliver us all over the Metro area. As soon as we moved in we realized the benefits of living in a mixed-use city center with ample access to the amenities we need on foot. Also, we were centrally located which means we could get to most of the other city centers rather quickly on public transit. Density afforded us proximity. As Vicky Cheng explains, "The proximity of people and places brought about by both high building and people density offers a high degree of convenience for work, service and entertainment."[11]

I spent the first nine months simply exploring the city. I became acquainted with traversing the city on public transit, foot, or by bike. During that time our lone vehicle broke down which meant we were thrust into the world of relying 100 percent on transit. While it was not always fun, it was one of

---

[11] Ng, *Designing High-Density Cities*, 15.

the best things that could have happened to us. We learned to navigate the city as a family of five this way and did not take anything for granted.

During the first year I visited almost every city center to explore, walk, pray for and over it, and ask the Lord for discernment. We were praying that God would show us which places were the ones that resonated the most with us, as well as the places He wanted us to initially focus on. As we had numerous mission teams that would come up from the United States to visit and serve, I deployed them in various city centers to prayer walk and help us build relationships. Again, I was looking to see where God was already at work and where we could join him. Over time I felt compelled to work in several city centers, but two in particular initially. The first was Edmonds Town Centre where we lived. It was natural since that was where we were establishing relationships by simple proximity and repetition. The second was Lower Lonsdale in North Vancouver. It was about an hour away from us on transit, but we were quickly and easily making relational connections there.

First of all, my wife worked at a coffee shop there called JJ Bean. Immediately we began connecting with a group of young adults who lived on the North Shore through that employment opportunity. We learned quickly that the culture and demographics of the North Shore are significantly different than Edmonds Town Centre in Burnaby. The primary ethnicity in Edmonds is Asian while the primarily "visible minority" in North Vancouver is Persian.

Secondly, through our emerging outdoor adventure non-profit that I was attempting to launch, I was intentionally connecting with various companies and their owners. Several of these companies in particular happened to be in Lower Lonsdale. I would visit them on a regular basis as well as various other outdoor adventure stores ranging from Mountain Equipment Co-Op to bike shops and so forth. Next, I volunteered each week at the North Shore Neighbourhood House helping them develop a social media presence. They too were located in Lower Lonsdale. Lastly, we started the Red Couch, a campus ministry, at Capilano University in North Vancouver which was only five minutes away from JJ Bean. After our second meeting on campus we already had fifteen students.

It was an exciting time. All of these endeavors were focused and strategic to build our relational network in that city center. We did not have to be nearly as intentional in Edmonds since by simply living there we were regularly meeting lots of people and cultivating relationships. The relational network on the North Shore was rapidly expanding.

Through my relationship with the North Shore Neighbourhood House I was connected with most of the media outlets across the city. That brought me into contact and friendship with one of the reporters from the *North Shore*

Outlook. He was intrigued by what I was doing, my love for the city, and our involvement in making it a better place. He asked if he could write an article about me and church planting on the North Shore. Through our weekly coffee get-togethers at JJ Bean for the article, he not only heard my stories of working with the North Shore Neighbourhood House, the Red Couch, and our attempts at launching an outdoor adventure non-profit, but I shared with him the Gospel. The article that he wrote was called "A Fisher of Men—The Life of a Church Planter."[12] We felt that we were on the precipice for something amazing to happen. Everything was on an upswing and we were gaining momentum as we were trying to start our church from scratch.

Our approach was that of an urban missionary rather than a conventional church planter. That is to say, we started ministries and organizations, as well as volunteered, all the while seeding the cultural soil with good deeds and the Gospel to see a church someday sprout. In the words of Eric Swanson and Sam Williams, "Good deeds almost always produce goodwill with others. When people are observers or recipients of unmerited acts of kindness, they sit up and take notice."[13] They go on to expand on that thought in relation to the Gospel:

---

[12] Kolenko, "A Fisher of Men—The Life of a Church Planter."

[13] *To Transform a City*, 129.

> When the church defends the innocent, stands up to the evil in this world, and serves the community with good deeds, these actions often result in good will toward the church. Even people like Albert Einstein take note. But remember this—good will is not the same thing as good news. Winning the goodwill of the community should not imply that something of eternal, salvific significance has occurred! The goodwill generated by our actions provides an opportunity to share the good news about Jesus.[14]

That was certainly our approach. It was not a quick-growth plan for establishing a church. It was an imbedded missional-incarnational posture.

But as I've I alluded to already, we were not able to see our plans in Vancouver come to fruition. After nearly two years we had to leave Canada and move back to the United States. It is difficult to fully assess this church planting experience since we were still in the foundation-building stage and were planning for the long term. With that said, one of the lessons I learned, and sought to establish while there, was the need to take a team-oriented approach. This was my intention behind teaching for a seminary as well as launching new campus ministries. I knew I needed a growing group of leaders so I sought to build this team through the aforementioned ways. Another difficulty in this approach is the viability of this model as a career path for church planting. If the goal is to quickly grow a church that will pay the salary of the pastor-

---

[14] Ibid., 130.

Chapter 2

planter, this may not be the model for use as it requires more of a missionary posture.

Church Planting in a New City

After Vancouver we relocated six hours south of the border to Portland, Oregon. Like Vancouver, Portland is highly regard for its livability and active transportation options. While conducting research for my dissertation I had included Portland as one of my focus cities so I had spent time pouring over maps, church planting websites, and interviewing church planters. "Portland is a great model city for many because of its revitalized downtown core, investment in a light rail system, their land-use planning strategy, and the city's progress towards being an eco-friendly and sustainable city. With its abundance of gentrified neighborhoods full of coffee shops and microbreweries, Portland is a perfect city to study church planting in."[15] We transitioned from living in a dense city center, which was highly international and multicultural, to a lower-density inner-city urban neighborhood that is going through extensive gentrification. Any ideas of living a walkable lifestyle had been jettisoned partially because of our new neighborhood. Instead, Portland is a bike-friendly city. As Jeff Mapes in *Pedaling Revolution* points out, "Portland residents use the bike for transportation more than any other large city

---

[15] *Metrospiritual*, 13.

in America, and the city has gained an international reputation for encouraging bicycling."[16]

Portland, like Vancouver, is unique. It has its own creative urbanism. Levinson and Krizek in *Planning for Place and Plexus* write, "Many New Urbanists themselves often refer to Portland, Oregon, with its light-rail transit orientation and urban growth boundary, as their model city."[17] Both cities are held up as models for sustainable transit-friendly progressive cities in their overall urban form. Vancouver is well known for its dense city centers and Skytrain network. Portland is earning a global reputation for being bike-oriented as Heying points out in *Brew to Bikes*. "The bike network, combined with the city's transit system and planners' focus on developing amenities in neighborhoods allows people to access work, shopping, and social and recreation destinations without a car. Portland's emerging reputation for a car-free lifestyle is a significant draw for a new creative class, especially bike-related artisans."[18] As missiologists we recognize the different cultural milieu and adapt accordingly. Even though we were still in the Pacific Northwest, and only hours from Vancouver, the different cultural and urban realities called for a different approach to church planting.

---

[16] Mapes, *Pedaling Revolution*, 142-143.

[17] Levinson and Krizek, *Planning for Place and Plexus*, 231.

[18] Heying, *Brew to Bikes*, 110.

Chapter 2

To contend that Portland is a multi-nucleated city in the same way as Vancouver or even LA might be a stretch, but with progressive planning the city has charted a course for the future that involves a more robust transportation system and the creation and strengthening of so-called "20-Minute Communities." Wes Hughes, Urban Church Planting Catalyst for the Northwest Baptist Convention, has developed a church planting strategy called, "PDX20: Church Planting in 20-Minute Communities." He writes, "In keeping with Portland's progressive strategies for urban planning, the city has launched a new plan to increase development of '20-minute neighborhoods.' A 20-minute neighborhood is defined as everything a person needs for his or her daily life within an easy 20-minute stroll from home."[19] In an interview in *Fast Company*, former Portland Mayor Sam Adams says this about his dream of these 20-minute communities:

> We're also working to make every section of Portland a complete 20-minute neighborhood to strengthen our local economy. Two-thirds of all trips in Portland and in most American cities are not about getting to and from work. So if I can offer quality, affordable goods and services, eliminate food deserts, have neighborhoods with schools and parks and amenities—if I can create these 20-minute complete neighborhoods all over Portland—it strengthens our local economy.[20]

---

[19] Hughes, "PDX20: Church Planting in '20-Minute Communities."

[20] Carr, "Innovative Mayor Sam Adams Builds a Cleaner Portland."

According to the Portland Plan, a 20-minute neighborhood is:

> A place with convenient, safe, and pedestrian-oriented access to the places people need to go to and the services people use nearly every day: transit, shopping, quality food, school, parks, and social activities, that is near and adjacent to housing. In other words, a 20-minute neighborhood is another name for a walkable environment. We have used the term 20-minute neighborhood because we think it is easier to understand —it is where people go and get to in about twenty minutes."[21]

Similar to the city center concept in Vancouver, the primary characteristics of these 20-minute neighborhoods are: a walkable environment, destinations that support a wide range of daily needs (e.g., shops, jobs, parks, etc), and residential density.[22]

There is a great synthesis and synergy between what we were attempting in Vancouver and what Hughes is advocating in Portland. As a result, we have been embedding our lives here in Portland, learning the city's unique urban expression, and discovering what a contextualized church looks like here. One of the first realizations for our family is that we knew we

---

[21] City of Portland Bureau of Planning and Sustainability, "Status Report: Twenty-minute Neighborhoods," 2.

[22] Ibid.

needed to live in one of these 20-minute communities. If this is the direction of where the city is heading, then we want to be part of it.

This is a good time to transition to the next chapter where I will begin addressing the walkable church and pedestrian-oriented church planting. While these concepts were birthed in Canada they are quickly finding a home not only in cities like Portland, but in many other cities that I visit.

The Multi-Nucleated Church

Chapter 3

Foundation: Walkable and Pedestrian-Scale (The Hub)

The impetus behind walkable churches and pedestrian-oriented church planting came to me from some of my basic observations of the city in which I lived. While these concepts are not neat and tidy, they do provide the backbone for a new yet old way of doing and being the church. It is new in the sense that in our evolving transportation technologies we have mostly abandoned life on the pedestrian-scale. "The current 'default setting' for urban growth relies on the automobile to reach an ever-widening set of destinations."[1] We do not think twice about driving three blocks to the coffee shop instead of spending five minutes walking there. On the other hand, this concept is as old as the church.

---

[1] Levinson and Krizek, *Planning for Place and Plexus*, 2.

The Multi-Nucleated Church

Up until the era of tramways and automobiles, most people simply gathered for worship and experienced church life either on foot, on horseback, or by carriage. No one commuted multiple miles except for those living in more rural settings. The life of the church was synonymous with being walkable. It is no surprise that the proliferation of megachurches, whether in North America or elsewhere, is predicated on the use of the automobile. So what would church life look like if the car was removed from the equation?

Walkability (or bikeability) is not only a foundational idea for the church, but it also has wider-reaching applications for the overall health of dense urban contexts. "Pedestrian strategies enable each centre in a city to give priority to the most fundamental of human interactions: the walking-based face-to-face contact that gives human life to a city and, in the process, reduces ecological footprint."[2] In *View From the Urban Loft* I expanded on the concept of church planting on the pedestrian-scale and walkable or bike-friendly churches. "What if we could catch just a glimpse of how dense walkable neighborhoods, bike-friendly cities, and thoroughly public transportation could indeed increase the impact and influence of the church and at the same time promote values that are more Kingdom-minded than consumer-oriented. What if, indeed?"[3] Based upon these factors, processing how to go

---

[2] UN-HABITAT, *Global Report on Human Settlement 2009*, 127.

[3] Benesh, *View From the Urban Loft*, 160.

Chapter 3

about church planting and living in a dense city center, I began conceptualizing further what church planting in these hubs would look like. I labeled it "Pedestrian-Oriented Church Planting,"[4] which I spent a chapter expanding on in *View from the Urban Loft*.

"Pedestrian-Oriented Church Planting is starting walkable churches in dense neighborhoods that are accessible by foot, available for all local inhabitants (rich, poor, young, old, and different ethnicities), rooted in the community, and acts as lead catalysts in community transformation."[5] When it comes to pedestrian-oriented church planting, which assumes higher density cities, again, it is urban form that is dictating the *how* of church planting. "Doing ministry and church planting in this manner acknowledges three foundational realities: the built environment plays a shaping role (density), transportation influences the body life of a church (mobility), and theology of place is valued (city care)."[6] The reality is that in most parts of the city this form of church planting is not doable. If everyone lived on half-acre lots then this model becomes problematic. It necessitates urban density.

There are numerous benefits for focusing on the pedestrian-scale when church planting in the center of a

---

[4] I first shared this concept at *The Walkable Church* lecture on March 23, 2011, in Burnaby, BC.

[5] *View From the Urban Loft*, 165.

[6] Ibid.

multi-nucleated or polycentric city. Again, I will recount what I began formulating in chapter 15 of *View From the Urban Loft*. The conditions of polycentric cities create the right kind of environment for this kind of approach.

> I believe there are significant benefits to pedestrian-oriented church planting that are worthy of exploration. One such benefit is that it is accessible to all. Those who live in higher-density neighborhoods have more accessibility to your church and its body life. Socio-economics no longer is a dividing line, because people are not excluded because they can't drive to any of the gatherings. Pedestrian-oriented church planting has an aim to remove obstacles or barriers that may hinder various segments of society and make church life accessible to all.
>
> A second benefit to this mode of church planting is that it creates a natural rootedness in the neighborhood. If one of the identifying markers of a church is its auto-dependent commuting patterns, that can pose some serious threats to local involvement on the neighborhood scale.
>
> Another benefit of pedestrian-oriented church planting and walkable churches in denser urban environments is that the foundation of community is found in the communal. This builds off the second point in elevating rootedness in place. What I am highlighting is that a walkable church means that people are living within proximity of one another. When that is the case, then church life takes on a more communal element as there is a greater chance of spontaneous run-ins whether at the coffee shop, grocery store, library, and so forth.

Chapter 3

> A communal neighborhood-rooted element to church life forces us to deal with what community is all about. We're also forced to even be in community with people not like us or who we may not even like. A church that is rooted in a neighborhood has the opportunity to act as a lead catalyst in community transformation. When churches are walkable and neighborhood-focused, they can begin forming the backbone of transformation endeavors.[7]

While this is not an exhaustive list, it begins setting forth some of the positive benefits that result when the scale of church planting is reduced to being walkable or even bike-friendly.

What becomes immediately noticeable is that the scale is greatly reduced. Rather than conceptualizing a large regional church, these types of churches are not as fixated on growth as they are on multiplication. That does not mean that, given population density and the sheer number of those living in an area, that a large church is not possible, but again, too often large churches base their growth on auto-based commuting patterns. This is not wrong, and in many parts of the city this is the only way church planting can be done. The point is not to hold to some purist ideal about transportation technologies, but instead to let these same realities, along with urban form, influence the way church planting is to be done.

The more that I travel to other city centers across the continent the more I am pleasantly surprised to see how city

---

[7] Ibid., 165-170.

after city is aggressively implementing downtown revitalization strategies that include urban infill and densification, streetcars, bike lanes, and an overall pedestrian-oriented environment. The implications then for this chapter and this book are that this conversation is not reserved for places like Vancouver, inside the Loop in Chicago, or Manhattan. Even cities like Tucson or Phoenix or Houston are encouraging more people to move into the central city to live this kind of lifestyle. In other words, while many may consider it a novelty, the notion of pedestrian-oriented church planting is on the cusp of gaining significant momentum.

Already there is a shift underway with a flurry of thinkers, writers, and books all pointing in this direction. Books such as *The New Parish* by Paul Sparks, Tim Soerens, and Dwight Friesen, and *Slow Church* by C. Christopher Smith and John Pattison do a great job in reorienting our thinking to the smaller-scale walkable parish model which is the antithesis of the commuter- or consumer-based church. A growing number of people are *re-neighboring* their communities with this in mind. This is keeping in step with larger movements reshaping North American cities and the continued rise of localism. Walking and biking as well as public transit then are literally the vehicles for this lifestyle and way of doing and being the church.

Chapter 3

Walkable Churches and Movements

The irony of current church planting methodologies which cater to the automobile culture is that the only semblance of a church planting movement in North America happened before the advent of the personal automobile.

> Shortly after the United States won its war for independence, people began moving westward in great numbers. The population shift was massive—regions that had been virtually uninhabited in 1776 contained one-third of the nation's population by 1790. Wherever they went, a remarkable church planting movement swept through the American frontier. It resulted in multiple churches in virtually every county, city, town, and hamlet that settlers inhabited. The planting of new churches occurred at a rate that is almost unbelievable, especially because the blitz of church planting had no central hub.[8]

This took place without any training, any evangelistic or church planting programs or strategies, and professional clergy. What this tells us is that rapid church multiplication can take place on a low-key, informal, simple, and walkable scale. In some ways, these church networks were "multi-nucleated" in the sense that there was one leader who was networking, leading, and teaching at a multiplicity of sites. "Each of the Methodist circuits included twenty to thirty preaching points.

---

[8] Stetzer and Bird, *Viral Churches*, 50.

The Multi-Nucleated Church

Worship services were generally held in whatever facilities were available—even outside."[9]

While these circuit riders were mobile, thanks to the horse, the citizens of these frontier towns more than likely walked so they could access the body life of a church. Again, I am not holding onto some purist ideals of yesteryear or longing for the "good old days." I am simply making the observation that church planting movements can indeed take place without much of the trappings that we think are necessary for church life today. As Alan Hirsch comments,

> I have come to the unnerving conclusion that God's people are more potent by far when they have little of what we recognize as church institution in their life together. For clarity, therefore, there needs to be a clear distinction between necessary organizational structure and institutionalism. As we shall see, structures are absolutely necessary for cooperative human action as well as for maintaining some form of coherent social patterns. However, it seems that over time the increasingly impersonal structures of the institution assumes roles, responsibilities, and authority that legitimately belong to the whole people of God in their local and grassroots expressions."[10]

The impulse behind pedestrian-oriented church planting and walkable churches is to strip the church and church planting of all unnecessary encumbrances so it can free people

---

[9] Ibid., 54.

[10] Hirsch, *The Forgotten Ways*, 23.

Chapter 3

up to start simple networked churches across multi-nucleated cities. The importance of following this line of thinking and strategy in dense settings is that, because of its structural fluidity and adaptability, it allows for life in the body of Christ to form around urban expression. Also, as I mentioned earlier, since there is a resurgence of efforts to densify city centers and urban neighborhoods to make them more walkable and bike-friendly, it is paramount for church planting strategies to follow suit. Levinson and Krizek point out this shift in what is taking places in our city centers. "The conventional wisdom in turn-of-the-millennium urban planning urges tightly knitting land use and transportation together, preferably in compact developments containing diverse uses, which makes it easier to walk, bicycle or take transit and discourage driving."[11] It really then is not a stretch to begin adapting our church planting strategies accordingly.

As I mentioned in the Preface to the second edition, my role has changed since I first began writing this book in 2011. In the course of my travels and working with numerous urban church plants in cities across North America, I have spent time walking and biking around city centers such as Oklahoma City, Montreal, Quebec City, and Salt Lake City. What I read online in preparation for each trip and what I experience firsthand on the ground in each city is the common storyline of people migrating *en masse* back to the central city. Some

---

[11] *Planning for Place and Plexus*, 2.

cities are well on their way to being thoroughly gentrified while others are on the front end and others are seeing foreign immigrants moving in.

Neighborhoods that were once in decline are being revitalized through an influx of new residents. The church planters that I have worked with all have seen these trends; it is the primary reason why they are planting where they are. Many come from other cities or the suburbs. However, once rooted in the city, many have come to the realization that the context of planting churches downtown or in central city neighborhoods means that it is essential for them to re-conceive and rethink how to plant the Gospel and churches in these settings. What many admit is that life in the urban core (or polycentric hubs) is the reason why they are changing and adapting their strategies. This will be the focus of the next chapter.

Chapter 4

Life in a Dense Urban Setting

It's a challenge to write about dense urban settings because of the various ways this label applies from city to city whether in North America, Southeast Asia, Europe, South America, and so on. Here I'll attempt to begin defining, listing, and detailing what life looks like in these types of settings and in particular, in high-density hubs. With that established, we will revisit what church planting can look like there. I have already begun laying the foundation in terms of "Pedestrian-Oriented Church Planting." It will be my aim and goal to draw from a global urban framework rather than only from the experiences in the two cities I've written about thus far.

"You see them all over the world. More than a billion of us live in high-rises. But most of these low- and middle-income buildings are now aging and falling into disrepair."[1] This quote comes from an online interactive documentary called *One Millionth Tower*, which "re-imagines a universal thread of our global urban fabric—the dilapidated high-rise neighbourhood."[2] What the documentary highlights for our discussion is the struggle with defining urban versus suburban. No longer do these caricatures and labels always apply. Some of the stories of these high-rise are in high-density suburban settings whether Toronto, Canada, or Mumbai, India. I also noted this tension when I was doing my research for *Metrospiritual*:

> Another example would be from the vantage point of where I sat as I wrote this chapter, which was at a Waves Coffee in downtown New Westminster, BC. Although New Westminster is the oldest city in British Columbia and was the first capital of the province, today it is, more or less, considered a suburb of Vancouver. Vancouver acts as the main hub of the metro area with various suburbs radiating out from the center. However, the problem comes with how to define New Westminster or some of the other suburbs. While a city of only sixty thousand residents, the cultural markers would label it as a very urban place. There are two distinct districts, Downtown and Uptown, which are comprised of very compact residential and commercial high-rise cores. As far as central cities or downtowns go, New Westminster has a larger and denser downtown in its built environment than

---

[1] Cizek, "One Millionth Tower."

[2] Ibid.

two of the other focus cities in my project. But New Westminster is a suburb, or is it? On the City of New Westminster's website they even classify themselves as urban. When it comes to defining church planting how would I categorize a new church here? Urban? Suburban? Next to New Westminster and sitting in between it and Vancouver proper is Burnaby. Is that a suburb as well? There are four separate city centers, each comprising of compact central business districts full of high-rises. Even the smallest of the city centers has a greater skyline than the downtowns of many larger cities.[3]

As a result, I'm prone to refer to places as *high-density*, *low-density*, etc. The labels of urban and suburban do not always reveal key information about density, or the lack thereof.

What the *One Millionth Tower* shows is the difficulty of life in these sometimes faceless high-density environments. The director seeks to address the challenges and move the conversation forward in hopes of seeing change take place. "As we move into this century, we fundamentally lack a vision to successfully house the urban species. The world is rapidly urbanizing, and yet we are not planning ahead—we can't even keep up, and the Band-Aid solutions profit a few of us, exploiting the rest."[4] This goes hand-in-hand with what Glaeser writes: "On a planet with vast amounts of space we choose cities."[5] We are choosing to live in cities, and large

---

[3] Benesh, *Metrospiritual*, 64.

[4] "One Millionth Tower."

[5] Glaeser, *Triumph of the City*, 1.

dense cities at that. How do we envision a better urban future that benefits the rich and the poor? Again, for our perspective, where and how does church planting in these environments also help shape and form a better urban future?

At the end of Chapter 3 in his book *Triumph of the City*, Glaeser makes a bold statement, which he unpacks in the following chapter. It reveals the importance not only of cities, but of high-density contexts as well. "While poverty and urban failure are often linked in people's minds, particularly because declining places attract poor people with cheap housing, there's nothing intrinsically wrong with urban poverty."[6] In some ways this displays the other side of the discussion that the *One Millionth Tower* documentary reveals. In his next chapter, "What's Good About Slums?" Glaeser goes on give credence to the importance of cities, and I would add, to city centers in multi-nucleated cities. It is the density which offers urban advantage. He boldly states:

> The presence of poverty in cities from Rio to Rotterdam reflects urban strength, not weakness. Megacities are not too big. Limiting their growth would cause significantly more hardship than gain, and urban growth is a great way to reduce rural poverty. The seemingly equal world of the suburb is in many ways more of a problem for society as a whole, especially those people who can't afford its pleasures, than the unequal world of the city.[7]

---

[6] Ibid., 67.

[7] Ibid., 70.

Cities, especially its higher-density parts, get a bad rap. However, one of the reasons behind their magnetic draw is this urban advantage that density and proximity provide. Glaeser has a few more observations to make. First, cities, particularly high-density city centers, draw people to them because they offer them the hope of a better life. "Cities aren't full of poor people because cities make people poor, but because cities attract poor people with the prospect of improving their lot in life."[8] Next, these high-density city centers attract the poor because of various urban amenities, especially mass transit. "The great urban poverty paradox is that if a city improves life for poor people currently living there by improving public schools or mass transit, that city will attract more poor people."[9] Lastly, and this ties into his first point, these higher-density places in the city offer people a better economic outlook. "Two economists tried to understand the impact of building height on economic productivity by comparing area that had natural features like bedrock, which makes it cheaper to build up, with areas where building up was naturally more difficult. They found that labor productivity and wages were significantly higher in those places where density was easier to develop."[10]

---

[8] Ibid.

[9] Ibid., 71.

[10] Ibid., 142.

Now let us transition to dealing more specifically with life in these high-density city centers. There are numerous characteristics of these types of high-density urban environments that favor a more walkable lifestyle. "According to the research, walkable environments—or 20-minute neighborhoods—generally include the following:

- building scales that are comfortable for pedestrians;
- mixed-use and dense development near neighborhood services and transit;
- distinct and identifiable centers and public spaces;
- a variety of connected transportation options;
- lower speed limits on streets;
- accessible design; and
- a street grid or other frequently connected network of local streets.[11]

"High building density, therefore, helps to reduce the pressure to develop open spaces and releases more land for communal facilities and service to improve the quality of urban living."[12] If done well, compact walkable areas can be very beneficial for the city and residents alike. However, what the *One Millionth Tower* documentary reveals is that when done poorly, these same kinds of places can lead people to lives of quiet and unseen desperation.

---

[11] City of Portland Bureau of Planning and Sustainability, "Status Report: Twenty-minute Neighborhoods," 3.

[12] Ng, *Designing High-Density Cities*, 14.

Some of the other characteristics of these types of settings may or may not apply to all world-class cities across the globe. I am well aware that a characteristic such as dense multiculturalism is not applicable to all cities. With that said, I believe some of the common characteristics of high-density environments are as follows: dense multiculturalism, higher dependency on public transit, greater socio-economic mixing, cultural preferences for higher-density places (a lifestyle choice), access to amenities, and urban advantage and higher creativity. This is certainly not an exhaustive list, nor is it representative of all places and cities which are characterized by high density. I will briefly unpack each point on the list.

Dense Multiculturalism

A distinct advantage that high-density districts offer is the reality of dense multiculturalism. Oftentimes this phenomenon is most evident in these contexts. Due to density and proximity, this dynamic is more readily noticeable because there are more people populating the area in comparison to low-density areas. Again, these are simply generalizations with many exceptions based upon the large list of global cities. For example, Canada's urban fabric reveals a classic example of dense multiculturalism. Sociologist Harry Hiller points out, "Without doubt, major Canadian cities are experiencing unprecedented growth in racial and ethnic diversity, which is largely a result of immigration. Immigrants and their adaptation process have become integral components of understanding Canadian cities."[13] He adds, "Since most recent immigrants have come from diverse countries, especially from non-European countries, and since most of them have settled in major cities, the Canadian urban landscape has become dramatically diverse in recent decades."[14]

Even here in Portland one can get a sense of denser multiculturalism in higher-density parts of the city, but it is not uniform across the city. In fact, due to its changing landscape as a result of gentrification, many diverse parts of the city are now in sprawling lower-density areas. Sometimes, due to sheer numbers, we notice multiculturalism more when there is a higher concentration of people in a given place. It also highlights the challenges of planting churches in such a setting. "One of the greatest challenges to reaching our cities with the gospel is finding ways of reaching the vast array of cultures that inhabit our cities."[15]

Higher Dependency on Public Transit / Walkability

"Having the option of walking to our daily destinations not only improves the quality of our lives and deepens our experiences of community, it also connects us to the biblical

---

[13] Hiller, *Urban Canada*, 132.

[14] Ibid., 140.

[15] Patrick and Carter, *For the City*, 71.

setting where walking was a part of life."[16] This is certainly an advantage not just for the poor, but for the rich as well. As we looked at previously, Glaeser points out that investment in public transportation draws more poor people to urban areas. On the other hand, it also pulls in the rich who desire to live a more urban lifestyle and get around by foot, on bike, streetcar, light rail, and so forth.

Regardless of socio-economic status, the appeal of good public transit attracts people from a wide variety of backgrounds to higher-density environments. For the purposes of our discussion, I am lumping bicycle transportation into the equation as Portland continues to push the envelope and lead the charge nationally in this area. However, what this also highlights is the social tension that certain transportation technologies can bring. Here is how this breaks down and what this looks like in Portland. Everyone uses light rail. Many prefer to commute into the CBD this way to avoid paying for parking. This is a highly acceptable and socially normal mode of public transit. However, that's not the case with the bus system.

The common perception of those who ride the buses are low-income and ethnic minorities. The bus is a common fixture and necessity for many who depend on it to get around in the city. For those who can afford it, the car is still preferred outside of high-density contexts. Lastly, the bicycle as a mode

---

[16] Jacobsen, *Sidewalks in the Kingdom*, 95.

of transportation is just as highly segmented and segregated along social-class lines in some circles even though that continues to change. I have heard from numerous people that the dividing line looks like this: to ethnic whites, especially young urban hipsters, the bicycle is not only doable, but very desirable. For many in this category, it is the preferred mode of transportation and the new status symbol in sustainable transportation. In some way, it almost carries with it an elitist mentality and exclusivity: There are those who bike and then everyone else. On the other hand, many ethnic blacks have told me that the bicycle carries a certain perceived stigma that is neither good nor desirable from their point or view. For them the bike is a symbol of poverty because they can't afford a car. Portland State University professor Karen Gibson asks, "Portland is lauded for its livability—but livability for whom?"[17]

A of these transportation options … bicycle, bus, streetcar, light-rail, and foot … all presuppose urban density. Without density these modes of transportation could not be supported. "Ideas about compact and transport-based cities are ways in which cities could impact less upon climate change. Retrofitting existing car-based cities with public transport– and pedestrian-based movement systems would go a long way towards reducing fuel demands. It has also been suggested that cities planned in this way are more equitable in terms of

---

[17] Gibson, "Bleeding Albina," 4.

Chapter 4

providing good accessibility to both wealthier and poorer urban residents and overcoming spatial marginalization."[18]

Greater Socio-Economic Mixing

Higher-density city centers offer what oftentimes the low-density suburbs lack, namely a diverse socio-economic mixing. In a typical subdivision, the houses are within a certain price range which means those who buy them have to fall within a certain income bracket to be able to afford it. It creates a very homogenous socio-economic grouping. On the other hand, in the city oftentimes there can be low-income housing across the road from middle- to upper-class housing. Sometimes they even coexist in the same building. We saw this reality in Edmonds Town Centre where affluent middle-class Chinese lived in high-rise towers across the street from lower-income Iraqi refugees in four-story, low-quality apartments. People on one side of the street drove BMWs and Mercedes while those on the other side walked everywhere with their pull-along carts. Certainly on some levels this could be problematic, but there can also be a beauty in such mixing.

"In the first place, it allows people from different income levels to live near each other and interact with each other."[19] It is precisely these dynamics which create the urban advantage of these dense areas with diverse ethnicities and socio-

---

[18] UN-HABITAT, *Global Report on Human Settlement 2009*, 14.

[19] *Sidewalks in the Kingdom*, 92.

economic groupings. These dynamics tie into the first characteristic of dense multiculturalism. "Immigration is also essential to urban success. The growth of New York and Chicago over the past two decades is largely due to the hundreds of thousands of immigrants who have come to those cities. Cities are good for immigrants and immigrants are good for cities."[20] That is true regardless of their socio-economic status.

Cultural Preference for Urban Living

Another reason why people live in high-density urban contexts is precisely because they prefer it. At the heart of this are cultural preferences and backgrounds that can certainly play a shaping role. For example, groups of people who grew up overseas in dense urban environments make the transition to similar contexts in North American cities easier than those who did not grow up in such an environment. Let me explain. In many parts of the world having multiple generations living together in one dwelling is normative. In some cases this can lead to tighter living conditions. On the other hand, in the US, where space is abundant, people tend to live in much larger houses, even in the city. It sometimes seems as though low-density suburbs, as a cultural preference and value, are synonymous with being an American. We value our space. As a result, it takes more to woo Americans to give up their 2,500

---

[20] *Triumph of the City*, 252.

square-foot suburban ranch-style home in the suburbs in favor of a fourth-floor 950square-foot condo or apartment in the city. But that seems to be changing.

An article entitled "Most Americans Want a Walkable Neighborhood, Not a Big House" starts off by highlighting Americans' changing mentality. "Six in 10 people also said they would sacrifice a bigger house to live in a neighborhood that featured a mix of houses, stores, and businesses within an easy walk."[21] What the article reveals is the growing appeal among Americans for these denser, walkable neighborhoods. It is at this intersection, be it the 20-minute neighborhood or the city center concept, where church planting makes a lot of sense. Indeed church planters need to embrace this growing trend.

Among immigrants and native-born citizens alike, there is a growing preference for an urban lifestyle which centers around public transit, walkability, and bikeability. This cultural preference reveals that the desire for density means a desire for the available amenities. "Decisions about where to live and work, although informed by habitual behavior, are made a dozen or so times over a lifetime. What mode of transportation to take—transit, automobile, or walking—tends to be habitual and informed by upbringing, personal

---

[21] Aronowitz, "Most Americans Want a Walkable Neighborhood, Not a Bike House."

preferences, and individual tolerance or being inconvenienced."[22] This leads us to our next point.

Access to Amenities

The genius behind high-density living is having various amenities within walking or biking distance. This is where a car-free lifestyle is not only doable, but favorable. This stands in stark contrast to the lower-density suburban settings. For example, where I live I can walk to a myriad of coffee shops, cafes, and restaurants. We also live directly above a branch of the Multnomah Public Library. It's a short walk to the light rail station, plus on bike I have quick and easy access to even a wider variety of amenities. This is in contrast to where my meeting was today. I biked an hour over the bridge from Portland into Vancouver, WA. Once across the river there is the perception that it's not as bike-friendly as Portland. I am sitting in a coffee shop in a classic yet trendy strip mall. To the extent that I can peer out of its giant windows, I cannot see any sort of housing or residential neighborhood. It seems that the only way to get here is to drive. I biked it but it is not a bike-friendly city. Whereas in Portland, I could park my bike out front of coffee shops with scores of other bikes, here mine is the lone bike outside. Density means access to amenities and for a growing population this is a desirable lifestyle choice.

---

[22] Levinson and Krizek, *Planning for Place and Plexus*, 97.

More and more Americans are opting to simply park their cars and leave them at home. Instead, many are (re)discovering the joys, freedom, and opportunities of living car-free which most often necessitates density. Where the church falters in this regard is we have yet to adapt accordingly. As a whole we are still planting churches and building our strategies based on the proliferation of a car-based lifestyle. Transitioning to compact urban environments means the church must recalibrate the way to do and be the church in a way that is reflective of this changing reality. Context determines the *how* of church planting and community transformation.

The Industrial Revolution, combined with the Enlightenment, paved the way (no pun intended) for a growth in the individualism shown in transportation preferences. "The urban growth stimulated by the market flourished amidst religious schism and was characterized by individualism and utilitarianism."[23] This meant that most people chose to drive because it truly is the most convenient and quickest way to get around. However, those trends are slowly changing as cities continue to go through a metamorphosis and embrace the new creative economy that is altering the urban landscape.

More and more people are eschewing low-density suburban sprawl in favor of denser urban contexts. In light of that, place continues to grow in importance whether personally or economically. Dense urban places provide access to a

---

[23] Bartholomew, *Where Mortals Dwell*, 255.

growing list of amenities which make these places desirable. "So when we choose a place, we're not only selecting a physical location—we're also picking the bundle of goods and service that will be available to us there."[24] Glaeser echoes this sentiment when he writes, "As humankind becomes wealthier, more people will choose their locations on the basis of pleasure as well as productivity. To understand why cities are succeeding and whether they will continue to thrive in the future, we must understand how urban amenities work and how consumer cities succeed."[25]

Urban Advantage

"The first thing that anyone notices on entering a city is the concentration of people and their activities. Simple as it is, this density has been little understood, and its benefits are too often squandered through the low-density development of cities today. The density of cities is their most basic advantage over any kind of settlement. Without density of settlement, most of what we learn, produce, construct, organize, consume, and provide as a service in the world would simply be too expensive. Density increases the sheer efficiency by which we can pursue an economic opportunity."[26] One of the dominant

---

[24] Florida, *Who's Your City?*, 11.

[25] *Triumph of the City*, 119.

[26] *Welcome to the Urban Revolution*, 27.

themes that I've raised, and will continue to bring up, is this concept of urban advantage that comes through proximity and clustering. Not only do manufacturing plants and business firms benefit from these agglomeration dynamics, but so do people who live in dense urban contexts.

Agglomeration economies influence where firms and businesses locate within cities. "Economists have speculated that this concentration of economic activity may be explained by cost or productivity advantages enjoyed by firms when they locate near other firms."[27] There are clear advantages for clustering. The same applies to people clustering together. Greenstone, Hornbeck, and Moretti note that, though the costs of living or operating businesses in higher density settings are greater than in other areas, these clustering dynamics are more important than ever before. "The possibility of documenting productivity advantages through agglomeration is tantalizing because it could provide insights into a series of important questions. Why are firms that produce nationally traded goods willing to locate in cities such as New York, San Francisco, or London that are characterized by extraordinary production costs? In general, why do cities exist, and what explains their historical development? Why do income differences persist across regions and countries?"[28]

---

[27] Greenstone et al, "Identifying Agglomeration Spillovers," 537.

[28] Ibid.

The clustering dynamics cannot be overlooked for the overall health and prosperity of the city ... and local citizens. "Modern cities are far more dependent on the role that density can play in speeding the flow of ideas."[29] Density brings about greater diversity and make easier the spreading of ideas. "When mutually supportive activities are located in proximity to each other, their concentration has a further synergistic effect."[30] It is difficult to quantify precisely the benefits of density and clustering, other than we know they are instrumental to this notion of urban advantage. We know ideas spread easier in these settings, people's lives "rub off" on one another, and so forth in this synergistic effect. "Ideas move from person to person within dense urban spaces, and this exchange occasionally creates miracles of human creativity."[31]

This is instrumental to understanding these high-density settings if we are to effectively plant churches and bring about community transformation. By highlighting some of the various elements of living in these kinds of settings it brings to the surface issues to which church planters and missiologists can not only respond accordingly, but can also design methodologies around these urban realities. In light of that, in the next chapter I will continue to explore further what church planting in these hubs looks like (or could look like).

---

[29] Glaeser, and Gottlieb, "The Wealth of Cities," 983.

[30] *Welcome to the Urban Revolution*, 28-29.

[31] *Triumph of the City*, 19.

Chapter 5

Church Planting in Multi-Nucleated Hubs

Now that we have explored life in high-density urban settings, as well as began exploring such topics as pedestrian-oriented church planting and walkable churches, I will now set forth some basic steps to move forward the discussion of planting in these places. It has been my contention throughout this book that urban form dictates the *how* of church planting. To neglect a city's overall urbanism is lazy missiology. It is too easy to become enamored with a certain style or methodology and seek to apply that template in all settings and contexts. With that said, as in the previous chapter, I will work through and expand on what church planting can look like in high-density (or *higher*-density) urban environments. But before that, a word of caution.

This is not as much a cautionary tale as it is an appeal for us to be cognizant of the culture and urban form in our cities.

Both are truly moving targets. Given how rapidly cities are changing both in culture and urban form, our role as missiologists is always ongoing. There will never be a moment where we "figure out" a city or neighborhood because in five years the whole neighborhood could flip. A white neighborhood could become Hispanic. A black neighborhood could become white. A district full of warehouses and vacant lots could be redeveloped into a trendy entertainment district.

I repeatedly use Tucson as an example for many things since it is a city that I know well ... or that I *knew* well. When we moved away from this sun-kissed Sonoran desert city the downtown was still only a place for government jobs, a transient population, eclectic stores, and scary, grungy businesses like Shot In the Dark Cafe with its frequent displays of obscene artwork on the walls. For decades Tucson citizens heard about different attempts to revitalize this sprawling city's urban core and all of the money pumped in to make it happen. Yet for many there was never any noticeable change. The few mainstay restaurants served the daytime business community or the robust number of government employees who worked downtown. Then my family and I moved away.

When I returned just five years later (which was a year ago now), I was dumbfounded by not only how much had changed, but also by the momentum of change that was building mass. All of a sudden (to me) the downtown had a

Chapter 5

streetcar and bike lanes. New housing and restaurants had popped up with even newer ones coming in. In only five years significant cultural changes as well as improvements in the built environment had taken place. For the sake of this conversation, therefore, either side of this five-year window would require a different church-planting strategy. Even the downtown population now has a growing number of housing options for college students and other Millennials who desire to live a pedestrian-oriented urban lifestyle.

So what does it look like to plant in central city neighborhoods and/or multi-nucleated hubs? The principles in this chapter in fact apply to denser urban settings regardless of whether the city is polycentric or not.

Simple

Start Simple and Small / Missionary vs. Church Planter

There are numerous issues and considerations that high-density urban contexts bring to the fore. In a highly complex environment, it is my belief that the best way to begin moving forward is counterintuitive: *start simple*. Simple in the sense of methodologies and strategies, but also simple in outlook and even how one views one's self. Maybe a foundational question in this regard is whether one views one's self as a church planter or a missionary. Each label brings with it a completely different outlook, orientation, and even existence. My bias leans towards adopting the posture of a missionary in these environments, but I also admit that this does not necessarily have to be everyone's overriding template.

This is something that I have personally wrestled with for years. It is a theme that continually surfaces in some of my writings as I flesh this out in the context of calling and giftedness:

> Something must change not only in regards to the way church planting is to be done in dense urban contexts, but also in the type of person the lead planter is. In many of our assessments systems we are still determining success or viability based upon still the entrepreneurial Type-A up-front charismatic personality. Many church planters already do not fit into that mold and when complex urban environments are brought into the equation, it can create tension. I suppose one of the key differences is in how church planters even see themselves: church planter or missionary.[1]

I continued to explore this dichotomy:

> One of the foundational questions that church planters ought to ask themselves is simply, "How do I see myself?" Do people see themselves as church planters or missionaries? The way that question is answered will often times be telling of the focus of their activities. Church planters most often would see the locus of their endeavors as starting a worship gathering. They are called church planters. Their initial funding and end goal would be for them to start some type of gathering for worship and instruction. That becomes the central focus of their

---

[1] Benesh, *Metrospiritual*, 159.

Chapter 5

energies and involvement in their community. Start a church and grow it. Leaders in this category see themselves as bible teachers, preachers, pastors/shepherds, organizers, administrators, and the like. Again, I am referring to broad and wide sweeping categories and generalizations.[2]

The reality is that, as Darrin Patrick and Matt Carter state, "The calling to reach our cities is bigger than any of us."[3] Patrick goes on to explain the importance of mobilizing the church to think and act like missionaries in their own neighborhoods. "A church for the city will release everyday missionaries loose into their neighborhoods so that they can bring their neighbors a taste of gospel-centered community."[4]

Starting small and simple just might begin with asking the question, "How would a missionary act in this setting?" That lone question can open up a series of other questions and ultimately a new lifestyle. This step-by-step process starts off small ... and simple. What is ironic is that this admonition to simplify mirrors what is taking place culturally. "Scores of practitioners, politicians, and professors claim that designing communities which more closely resemble built environments of centuries ago will allow households to live simpler, easier,

---

[2] Ibid., 109.

[3] Patrick and Carter, *For the City*, 176.

[4] Ibid., 97.

higher quality, and altogether copacetic lives."[5] Not only that, but we are in the midst of the *slow food* revolution where we're more in touch with our food and value when it is locally sourced. As well many are opting for all sorts of other local-sourced products. Doing church this way is a cultural fit.

In building off a play on words that fits this motif, Rick Shrout labels these new kinds of missionaries as "street crossers." As he explains, "First of all, street crossers are ministers of the gospel. They are not jaywalkers, because they cross streets at appropriate times and places. They look for the signals and pay close attention to them. They are aware of the law of the land and the lay of the land on the other side of the street. They understand that the land they seek to enter across the street is different from the land and culture from which they come."[6] Sometimes the simplest act of embodying a missionary posture is merely to cross the street, the hallway, or some other physical, racial, socio-economic demarcation to get to the other side.

Praying

Praying Fervently Over the City

We cannot overlook the importance of praying over and for our communities. "*Don't* underestimate the power of prayer. *Do* pray often for your neighborhood. Among other benefits,

---

[5] Levinson and Krizek, *Planning for Place and Plexus*, 2.

[6] Shrout, *Street Crossers*, xiv.

prayer reminds you that the monumental task of reaching your neighborhood with the gospel is an act of the Spirit, not something that is ultimately your own human effort."[7] In looking at church planting movements (CPMs) globally, David Garrison concluded that prayer is one of the Ten Universal Elements found in CPMs regardless of location. "It is the *vitality* of prayer in the missionary's personal life that leads to its imitation in the life of the new church and its leaders."[8]

On a personal or human level, one of the benefits of prayer is that it links our hearts and lives with those we're praying for. Since we care enough to fervently pray for them and the neighborhood, it has the affect of deeply connecting us. We pray because we care and the more we pray the more we care, which causes us to pray more ... and the cycle continues and expands. Craig Ott and Gene Wilson conclude that, "Of vital concern should be the spiritual health and fervor of the initial disciples, leaders and churches. Fervent prayer and wide sowing of the gospel pave the way for church multiplication but cannot totally explain it, because similar efforts among other people groups do not always yield a church planting movement."[9]

---

[7] *For the City*, 99.

[8] Garrison, *Church Planting Movements*, 33.

[9] Ott and Wilson, *Global Church Planting*, 73.

The Multi-Nucleated Church

Adapting

Let Urban Form Determine Methodology

"Cities are the epicenter of God's earthshaking movements today, and it's important that any model for starting new churches takes into account the unique nuances of ministry in an urban context."[10] That thought is pivotal and even the foundation of this book as it's my contention that we must engage in urban mission and church planting based upon urban form. We take in the context of the city we dwell in and let that shape the parameters of how we engage in mission.

Again, high-density neighborhoods require a significantly different approach which incorporates the rhythms of all the issues that we've explored here. It forces us to observe and ask questions. Is this area walkable? What is the primary way that people get around? How do people gather? Is it normative to have people over to one's home or do people mostly meet up in public places? How much of one's neighborhood is commercial versus residential? How much of it is mixed-use? What are the rhythms of this part of the city? Do businesses close early? What kind of nightlife is there? Are there a lot of families or very few? Observing urban form will reveal much. Then we can adapt our methodologies accordingly.

---

[10] *For the City*, 26.

Chapter 5

Relational

Be Relationally-Driven rather than Marketing-Driven

Another factor to consider in high-density urban contexts is the need to be relational. Urban denizens are bombarded with marketing from various platforms, whether social media, print, signage, email spamming, and so on. Many have become desensitized to these tactics where it simply becomes like background noise. What is missing is the relational ... the personal. We cannot underestimate the value of connecting by simply being present.

> Becoming embedded in a community is a long-term process. Lots of simple acts of kindness, smiles, and being courteous repeated countless times do not produce immediate measurable results. If the end goal is to quickly plant a church, therein lies the rub, in that this posture does not quickly amass a group of disenfranchised Christians who are looking for a hipper and trendier version of the church they now belong to or which they left some time ago. The impulse to be missional through and through is more than a pragmatic difference in approach or methodology; rather it becomes a complete reorientation of a way of life that seeks to live as a church (individually and collectively) with an outward trajectory.[11]

This goes back to the notion of being simple. Simple and relational are interconnected. Here the pace of church planting slows down and is boiled down to its simplest form: smiling at

---

[11] Benesh, *View From the Urban Loft*, 173.

the checkout clerk at the grocery store, starting up a conversation and leaving a big tip at the coffee shop, helping a mom carry groceries, volunteering to be a reader in an elementary school, and so much more. None of these things demand or require a marketing process. It simply takes simplicity and intentionality.

Serving

Seek the Welfare of the City through Acts of Kindness

Serving becomes synchronized with the previous topic of being relational to the point that ultimately it is a simple process. The more complex these high-density urban environments are the more it heightens the desire to strip away all of the noise and nonessentials. A simple approach is bathed in prayer, is open and adaptable to both urban form and the movement of the Holy Spirit, and is highly relational, which moves us into service. As we get to know our communities, develop a heart and passion for their overall well-being, through prayer we'll find ourselves jumping in to express this love through service.

We love and serve because we have been redeemed and transformed. This is an outflow of this inward transformation in our own lives. We love because we have been loved. We seek to redeem because we have been redeemed. We lay our lives down for the city because Jesus laid down his life for us.

Let the context of your city center, 20-minute community, or high-density urban setting determine where and how you serve. Templates and models are good to learn from, but each setting is unique and is shaped differently. The needs of a 20-minute community, like the Hollywood District in Portland, are different from Lower Lonsdale in North Vancouver, which is different from the Pudong in Shanghai, which is different from Canary Wharf in London. Context determines how we love and serve our cities.

Reconciling

Reconciliation (Bridging Race and Socio-Economics)

"Love compels us to give sacrificially to our family and work through difficult issues. It is the same with cities, and as they continue to diversify and internationalize through immigration, enlarge through urbanization, interconnect worldwide through globalization, and densify, it will at the same time bring about peculiar issues that low-density homogeneous settings simply do not have."[12] Reconciliation is a large overarching umbrella that covers a lot of territory. The good news of Jesus Christ is that life in him breaks down the walls. We are one in Christ ... rich, poor, European, African, Asian, Hispanic, Latino, and so on. In these types of urban settings reconciliation will always need to be at the forefront of what we are about. The subversive nature of the Kingdom of

---

[12] *Metrospiritual*, 158.

The Multi-Nucleated Church

God reorients everything. Kingdom values turn everything upside-down ... the first shall be the last ... the poor are blessed ... greatness is in servitude.

This reconciliation may be about creating a worshipping community that spans socio-economic lines which can be difficult to do. We have a lot of churches that may be multi-ethnic, but are still in the same socio-economic grouping. The challenge comes when a church is not only multicultural, but diverse socio-economically as well. It's in our nature that most of us like to hang out with those most like ourselves. The good news of the Kingdom of God, however, propels us in an outward pattern of loving and serving all. This good news has the power of reconciliation as we remember that the blood Jesus shed on the cross was of mixed-race blood.

Planting

Abundant Gospel Seed Sowing

The last point of church planting in these high-density urban hubs is the need for an abundance of Gospel seed-sowing. "So preaching the message of the kingdom, among other things, demands that we tell people through words and communicate with our action who this king is and what he values. *We tell an alternative story of life should be, can be, and one day will be.*"[13] Through a simple relational approach that is buttressed by loving and serving our community, we seek to

---

[13] Swanson and Williams, *To Transform a City*, 74.

abundantly sow the seeds of the good news of the Kingdom of God. Again, this is both proclaimed and embodied.

The goal of this chapter is not to be exhaustive, but to begin painting the picture of what church planting looks like (or can look like) in high-density urban contexts. Like everything else in church planting, context determines the how of church planting and mission. To take an extreme example, we would agree that missionaries would have to adapt how they engage in church planting on a remote jungle island in the South Pacific working with a primarily illiterate group of village dwellers. We would certainly contend that ministry would radically differ there compared with the high-density urban settings of Manhattan or Hong Kong. Context determines the how of mission. This chapter hopefully serves as not only a reminder towards that end, but also offers a way to begin developing a framework for engaging in church planting and mission in these urban places. The next chapter will explore how a multi-nucleated church stays inter-connected based upon the prevailing transportation technologies.

The Multi-Nucleated Church

Chapter 6

Function: Transportation-Centered Ecclesiology (The Spokes)

"The influence of twentieth-century land use-transportation planning and suburban development on the fabric of contemporary society, although systematically under-researched, has caught the attention of many and has been widely critiqued."[1] I echo that sentiment and also apply it to the role that transportation technologies play in shaping a church's ecclesiology. Throughout this book thus far I have attempted to point out the urban realities of high-density contexts and how they impact not only the life of those who live there, but also church planting in such places. In this chapter, I will explore the transportation spokes that connect the various hubs of the city. These same transportation options also connect the networked multi-nucleated church.

---

[1] Levinson and Krizek, *Planning for Place and Plexus*, 209.

The Multi-Nucleated Church

How a church connects and gathers *matters*. Geography is not dead. Last night I returned from training a newer church on the topic of gentrification. A sprawling sunbelt city, it is aggressively putting in multi-modal transportation options (e.g., streetcar, bike lanes, etc.) to encourage more people to leave their cars at home, as well as create an appealing and livable urban core in hopes of repopulating and revitalizing it. However, as almost all of the participants at the workshop admitted, they lived miles from where the church meets for worship. For many this posed a challenge simply to acknowledge this fact, let alone what it would mean for them to rectify it. You see, they desire and value the communal element that proximity affords, but auto-based commuting patterns have allowed for people in the church to live great distances from one another. Maybe some expression of a multi-nucleated church could help connect people better.

Transportation Infrastructure and the Church

The first concept that I will attempt to flesh out is in regards to connecting the multi-nucleated church via transportation. If urban form and transportation technologies shape how cities are laid out and influence the day-to-day lives of city dwellers, how cognizant of these foundational realities as part of the life of a church are we? Does the church simply operate in its own vacuum, unaware, negligent, or ignorant of the built environment of the city? How much or how little should the church allow these factors to shape and influence the way church is expressed?

The church that I referenced above is certainly talking about this. It is my assumption that even as little as three years ago the subject was not even on their radar. Many other churches that I have worked with are also wrestling through the implications of transportation and what that means for church life. Some churches are adding bike parking and promoting bicycling to gatherings, others are strategically placing their gathering locations along transit stations, and others are actively getting involved in advocacy groups and civic boards in their cities to promote multi-modal transit.

The built environment of the city and its transportation technologies influence the church in significant ways, and in the same way that it influences people who live in the city. "Transportation technologies shape our communities, and modern sprawl is the child of the automobile."[2] As we have explored earlier in the book, each wave of transportation innovation, in North America as well as globally, has shaped and reshaped the lives of those who live in these cities. Each wave allowed people to move farther and farther from the central city as cities evolved from walking to streetcars to autos. Now many of these cities are trying to retrofit these same central cities. However, the growth is still centrifugal

---

[2] Glaeser, *Triumph of the City*, 167.

because of these transportation realities. "Like omnibuses and streetcars, the automobile reshaped urban America."[3] And yet to counter that, cities that are known for rapid sprawl like Phoenix, Houston, or Tucson, are putting in streetcars, light rail and bike lanes to rectify and reshape their cities.

The neighborhood I now live in sits just outside Portland's CBD. It got its start before the twentieth century as transportation technologies allowed people to move away from the downtown core. "During the early 20th century Portland expanded rapidly on the east side of the Willamette River. At the start of this era the Hollywood District contained only a few homes and dirt roads. In 1906 a streetcar line ran the length of Sandy Boulevard."[4] With a density lower than the downtown, it is still compact and mixed-use. According to the website *Walkscore*,[5] it scores 95 out of 100 possible points for its walkability, making it the second-most walkable neighborhood in metro Portland.

The reason for the community's growth outside of the city center was because the streetcar line ran right through the heart of it. People could live outside of the congested downtown and still commute to work. As a result, while dense to a certain degree, it did not require the density that is most

---

[3] Ibid., 174.

[4] Portland State University Senior Capstone and Multnomah County Library, "Hollywood Neighborhood History."

[5] www.walkscore.com

often found in the CBD. This is reflective of the progression in changing transportation technologies:

> Each successful new type of transportation generally goes through three phases. First, technological breakthroughs enable large-scale production of a faster way to move, such as a steam-powered train or car. Second, a new transportation network is built, if needed, to accommodate this new technology. Third, people and companies change their geographic locations to take advantage of this new mode of transport.[6]

So how does a multi-nucleated church stay interconnected via transportation? This comes down to city-by-city scenarios because no two cities are alike and no two cities are equal in this regard. While Seattle has the monorail, a new modern streetcar, and a new light-rail connecting the airport with the downtown, the city is still heavily dependent upon the automobile. Also, the city has struggled because seemingly none of these transportation technologies connect or overlap (even though that is quickly changing). "Interestingly enough, the Monorail and the Light Rail were not even coordinated with each other, much less integrated; though they served different communities (the Monorail connecting the northwestern and southwestern areas with downtown, LRT[7] connecting northeastern and southeastern areas), it sometimes

---

[6] *Triumph of the City*, 168.

[7] Light Rail Transit.

seemed as if they were in direct competition."[8] These transportation options are really only available for a small segment of the population who live downtown.

Portland has worked more aggressively to ensure that a larger swath of people have access to the streetcars, the light-rail, and bicycle infrastructure, but even then it is not expanding fast enough. Lastly, where I used to live in Tucson, Arizona, it was almost exclusively a car-based city. With the new modern streetcar and added bike lanes, the city is attempting to retrofit the central city. However, like most cities, especially the sprawling sun belt cities, an auto-based lifestyle is nearly unavoidable. For our purposes in this book, how do the transportation realities in polycentric cities make it possible for a multi-nucleated church to stay interconnected? Also, how can this be more of a template as cities across North America not only densify in the city center but build up these clusters throughout their metro areas?

Much about a city's transportation infrastructure is more than simply varying technologies to transport people from Point A to Point B. This infrastructure most often forms a key role in the identity of the city.

> The stakes in major infrastructure developments are high; the identity of a city often hinges on them. The more distinctive the infrastructure, the stronger the identity. It is difficult to visit New York without encountering the

---

[8] *Planning for Place and Plexus*, 252.

subway. One rarely sees a movie filmed in San Francisco without an iconic image of cable cars on that city's steep streets. Residents and visitors alike in London lament that, as of December 2005, the famous Routemaster double-decker red buses have been withdrawn from regular service, leaving only two heritage routes for nostalgia's sake. Transportation systems are living monuments to their cities and contribute to the image the city wishes to project.[9]

As missiologists, then, it makes sense to form our ecclesiology around a city's transportation infrastructure while at the same time we draw principles from the New Testament. Along with adapting to culture as missionaries seek to do, our ecclesiology is upholding and valuing what the city values, namely its modes of transportation, upon which it builds its identity. Portland certainly has carved out its own niche in the United States as well as globally with its seemingly ubiquitous bicycle infrastructure and ever-growing streetcar and light-rail lines.

If life in the city centers or hubs are marked by walkability and overall pedestrian-oriented usage, then the spokes that connect these hubs are pivotal for us to study and understand. The premise of the multi-nucleated church ecclesiology rests on the ability for these hubs, 20-minute communities, or city centers to connect with one another. Where this varies from city to city is transportation technologies. In some cities, vast numbers may live a pedestrian-oriented lifestyle which means

---

[9] Ibid., 254.

the way to connect with other hubs is by bicycle, on foot, or via mass transit. For other cities, while those technologies are in place, for quickness and ease, many may still opt for connecting by auto. The goal is not to purport some purist neo-utopian urban existence, but instead to let transportation technologies shape how and where church is done.

In Portland, if one lives in the downtown core, inner SE, inner NE, or NW, this concept of interconnectivity through mass transit or bikeability is a doable reality. In other words, density is the overriding influential factor. Density also means more transportation options since this is where the streetcars, light-rail, and more robust bicycling networks are available in the city. Where this framework becomes problematic is in the lower-density parts of the city. With that said, the scope of this book hones in on church planting in the higher-density parts of the city. The body of church planting material available today has a low-density or suburban bias which means there are ample concepts, templates, and models to chose from for those types of settings. However, in the higher-density parts of the city we are still struggling because we attempt to implement strategies, models, templates, and methodologies that were created in the suburbs or low-density areas.

Where this conversation becomes challenging, as we look towards the future, is through urban revitalization projects and gentrification that are making central cities safer and more desirable than ever before. Historic minority neighborhoods

Chapter 6

where low-income families collected to live close to the CDB with access to jobs, services, and mass transit, are now becoming affordable only for the middle class.

Yesterday, in a coffee shop in such a neighborhood, I struck up a conversation with a computer animator who works for *Yahoo!* He used to live in this very neighborhood, but had to move out in order to find an affordable house to buy. Only a decade ago, the neighborhood was an African-American community with ample affordable housing stock. That same housing stock is now unaffordable to those who have been in this neighborhood for generations if they were to purchase a home today. This creates problems for those who are being displaced through renewal and gentrification. "The evidence of the poor becoming more and more isolated on the car-dependent urban fringe is very clear in Australia and increasingly so in North America as the focus of social policy has been on creating affordable housing on cheap land. The emphasis has not been on creating affordable housing in urban areas that is walkable, transit accessible, and energy efficient."[10]

In essence, in some cities the concept of a multi-nucleated church may seemingly become synonymous with being a hipster[11] church. On the other hand, in many other cities this

---

[10] Newman, et al., *Resilient Cities*, 50.

[11] Definition of hipster - "Hipsters are a subculture of men and women typically in their 20's and 30's that value independent thinking, counter-culture, progressive politics, an appreciation of art and indie-rock, creativity, intelligence, and witty banter." Urban Dictionary LLC, "Hipster."

kind of ecclesiology provides the framework of doing church equitably. Sometimes we fail to realize that at times our transportation choices in terms of how people gather for worship just may exclude some and only include those with the means to own and drive automobiles. The multi-nucleated church seeks to remedy that by being accessible to all within a geographic area.

What becomes difficult is setting forth the semblance of a template that affirms the unique nature of each and every city. What may work here may not work anywhere else. While it is easier to establish the framework of worshipping communities in these city centers or hubs, exactly how they stay connected to other worshipping communities in other hubs becomes more challenging. Based upon where I currently live, I have access to many of these 20-minute communities by light rail, and not all of them were even that walkable to begin with.

I am personally not limited to most of the rest of these hubs, since I do not mind riding my bike on typically rainy Portland days. This might be an option for a small few, but certainly not so for the majority. However, perhaps this then raises questions such as: how inter-connected are these various walkable worshipping communities in each hub? How often could or should we gather all of the hubs? Where would we? For what purposes?

The concept of the multi-nucleated church keeps the leaders more tightly connected, while the individual worshipping communities are more loosely connected. The particular dynamics of each city will form and shape this more than any of my hypotheses and assumptions. My goal in this book is to begin constructing a theoretical framework. As I explained at the outset, most books on the topic of church planting tend to be reverse-engineering rather than exploring a theoretical framework. Usually what happens is that a new church will explode with growth half-unexpectedly. Years or even decades later, after the leadership has been asked countless times how the church grew, they decide to write a book detailing what took place. This is reverse-engineering. If many leaders are honest about this, they would be the first to admit that they never imagined the church would take off like it did. In other words, they may have had a baseline strategy, but the Spirit carried them in an altered or completely different direction. Years later as they explain what took place they have to do some considerable reverse-engineering and begin teaching others to do what they did. This is how we get our template, modes, and models.

There is nothing wrong with this approach and most of us find it incredibly helpful to learn from others and glean from their experiences. However, where this becomes detrimental is that it hinders our ability to truly innovate and explore new terrain in church planting and ministry. As a result, I want to create a blueprint to build off of rather than do the opposite. This is not done to the exclusion of the work of the Holy

Spirit; nor is it an attempt to plan or strategize his presence or activity out of the church planting process. Rather, like a missionary or missiologist, this is an attempt to construct a framework of a church planting model that is predicated on the built environment of polycentric or multi-nucleated cities.

Chapter 7

Multi-Nucleated Ecclesiology

The theological and biblical basis for a theoretical framework of a multi-nucleated church is as old as the first-century church. More than likely, this framework was not at the forefront of the thinking of the early church, and I realize I run the risk of reading my own ecclesiological leanings into the New Testament. However, what we can learn, adapt, and adopt from Scripture is the fluidity with which the early church embraced by default as the Gospel rapidly expanded. My objective is not to proof-text, but simply to draw a few examples of how the early church structured its leadership that gives credence and credibility to a multi-nucleated church. Combined with the context of the city, I will explore what this urban ecclesiological framework looks like.

We find the first-century church was birthed in the urban cultural milieu of the day. "The church was birthed in the city,

The Multi-Nucleated Church

fled to other cities, and took root in the city."[1] Ray Bakke describes this birth of the church in regards to its scope and context. "Acts 2 reports the first hours of the church's existence as being both international and multilingual."[2] The city as context cannot be overlooked in investigating the early church. The first-century church had to adapt to life in the city and learn what it means to be this new covenant community in urban spaces. "As in the Gospel, the book of Acts invests theological significance in the city."[3] In *View from the Urban Loft*, I go on to describe the setting of the early church.

> The early church was birthed in the urban revolution, while the pace and reach of cities were on the upswing—the same trajectory that we are on today. Far from being born in a sleepy little backwoods village, the church put down its roots in a cosmopolitan city and continued in that same direction by taking root in even larger cities, culminating with the mega-city at that time, Rome. When we read the New Testament in its proper urban context, it acquires new depth and a wider appeal and application for Christians today who find themselves in cosmopolitan, pluralistic, multicultural environments. Jesus died and was resurrected just outside a city. And it was in that same city that the church was given life. It is

---

[1] Benesh, *View From the Urban Loft*, 96.

[2] Bakke, *A Theology as Big as the City*, 139.

[3] Conn and Ortiz, *Urban Ministry*, 129.

in that same urban context that the church today has the privilege of extending both common and saving grace.[4]

In light of this, the above-mentioned context forms the backdrop of our discussion of the multi-nucleated church. Because in the same way the city was the stage upon which the drama of the early church played out, the city is still the context of the global church. My point is not to create an overly complex system based upon a few passages in the New Testament, but instead to simply glean insights from a few examples.

Acts 20

In Acts 20, we find Paul speaking to the elders of the Ephesian church. What is readily noticeable are the hazy details of exactly what church life looked like. Where did the church meet? How often? What did they do when they met? How long did their gatherings last? Did they sing? What did the teaching look like? We are not sure, but what we do know is that Paul called together the elders of the Ephesian church to speak to them. "Now from Miletus he sent to Ephesus and called the elders of the church to come to him."[5] We are to assume there were a number of elders there, but were they all the leaders of one gathering? Or were there multiple churches

---

[4] *View From the Urban Loft*, 105.

[5] Acts 20:17.

or gatherings across Ephesus that the elders collectively oversaw?

Paul spoke to these elders, and what we immediately notice is a poignant detail about *how* the church gathered in Ephesus: "You yourselves know how I lived among you the whole time from the first day that I set foot in Asia, serving the Lord with all humility and with tears and with trials that happened to me through the plots of the Jews; how I did not shrink from declaring to you anything that was profitable, and *teaching you in public and from house to house*."[6] This is not a declarative statement about the need to go back and do house churches like they did in Ephesus and elsewhere. We notice that the whole church in Ephesus met in multiple homes, as well as publicly, and there were elders who oversaw these collective churches ... which in reality made up one church: the church in Ephesus.

One church, multiple locations, led by a group of elders. That is about all we can discern. We do know that these elders or overseers had responsibility to care for, shepherd, and guard this flock. "Pay careful attention to yourselves and to all the flock, in which the Holy Spirit has made you overseers, to care for the church of God, which he obtained with his own blood."[7] These overseers or elders had the collective

---

[6] Acts 20:18-20.

[7] Acts 20:28.

responsibility to care for the collection of gatherings that made up the church of Ephesus.

Conceptually, this is how the multi-nucleated church works. As churches multiply from hub to hub, city center to city center, and 20-minute community to 20-minute community, there is a group of elders or overseers who collectively lead, shepherd, care for, teach, and guard the church both in each location and collectively. I will resist making definitive statements about how *exactly* this looks because in each case it will be unique and adaptable based upon the prevailing circumstances. I surmise that each gathering will have at least one elder (depending on the size of the group) and each elder across the network will all be part of the larger team of elders or overseers. I hesitate to be exact about how many elders each gathering needs or even the number in the collective whole. This is highly fluid and adaptable. However, what becomes non-negotiable is *who* the elders themselves are and their qualifications. We see this detailed in 1 Timothy 3 and Titus 1. This leads to our next observation.

1 Timothy 3

Much ink has been used to write about 1 Timothy 3. There is ample scholarly work in this regard that is helpful to understand the nature of elders. Drawing attention to this passage here is not simply one more exercise of walking

The Multi-Nucleated Church

through the list of qualifications attribute by attribute. Instead, my purpose simply is to build off the previous discussion surrounding Acts 20. Wherever Paul went and churches were established he would immediately begin setting up leaders, elders and overseers. Do not lose the context. We find this back in Acts 14: "And when they had appointed elders for them in every church, with prayer and fasting they committed them to the Lord in whom they had believed."[8]

"It can be argued, then, that Paul's letters were addressed to urban Christians who were struggling with what it meant to now follow Jesus in the city. It was—and is—messy. People had plenty of pre-conversion baggage, regardless of whether they were Jew or Gentile. Each set of baggage was unique and posed a different set of challenges."[9] In many other ways as well the church adapted and adopted from culture. We find in numerous places the Greek word we usually translate as "church" can simply mean "assembly." It was used to describe anything from a meeting of a city's citizenry to an assembly of idol makers (Acts 19). The "who" defined what this assembly was about, whether it was citizens, the army, or the early covenant group of Jesus-followers. Context determined what "church" or "assembly" meant. How does this pertain to the conversation about elders?

---

[8] Acts 14:23.

[9] *View From the Urban Loft*, 102.

Chapter 7

In the culture of that day villages, towns, and cities all had elders: older men who gave oversight and wisdom to the people. While Paul was establishing new gatherings of those who were now followers of Jesus, we can assume he simply adopted and tweaked a structure that was already prevalent in that culture: town elders. However, what 1 Timothy 3 reveals is that those who bear the title of elder or overseer of the *church in Rome*, the *church in Ephesus*, the *church in Corinth*, were to be distinguished as being godly and wise. They also needed to have a good reputation among those outside these new covenant communities.

What does this mean for today's multi-nucleated church? Several observations can be made and applied. First, there is the need for it to be fluid and adaptable, drawing from the city and culture for insight. The early church constantly borrowed and adopted different elements from its surrounding culture. This was and is right, healthy, and normative. However, we also find throughout the pages of Paul's letters to these emerging churches where this was taken too far. "What was the nature of these collected epistles? They were letters written to urban Christians spread throughout the Roman Empire who were having difficulty understanding what it means to follow Jesus in the city."[10] But what Paul and the early church did was to adapt and adopt. The early church had elders because that was a normative social structure of the day.

---

[10] Ibid., 101.

The Multi-Nucleated Church

The second observation we can draw from 1 Timothy 3 is that these elders, as already noted, are to be godly men who have the character qualities to lead and oversee. While many argue that this term is used interchangeably with pastor or shepherd, I contend that they are indeed different. The elder or overseer is more of an "office" or "title" or "position," whereas pastor or shepherd has more to with a gift endowed by the Holy Spirit.[11] Regardless of how fluid or adaptable a multi-nucleated church is, there is always the need for godly leadership that is both positional (elder or overseer) and gifts-based (pastor, teacher, evangelist, etc.). First Timothy 3 gives us insight into who these elders are to be. It is my contention that Paul had co-opted the concept from the tradition of the village else. It is in his epistle to Titus that we find more information as to how these elders were dispersed throughout the church.

Titus 1

What is quickly apparent in the first chapter of this epistle is that Paul leaves Titus on the island of Crete to establish leadership for this new church. "This is why I left you in Crete, so that you might put what remained into order, and appoint elders in every town as I directed you."[12] The story I am most interested in exploring is what we find or can surmise

---

[11] This is simply my own ecclesiological leaning. I am not implying that a multi-nucleated church is predicated on the specifics of title, offices, and so on.

[12] Titus 1:5.

between the lines of this letter. My intention is not to create a complete leadership structure based upon a few remote, isolated, and unattached passages of Scripture. These are sample verses that highlight or reveal some of the underlying forces at play in the early church. When it comes to Paul's letter to Titus, there is a lot that can be learned simply by making a few simple observations.

We do not know the back story of the work of the Gospel on the island of Crete nor of the birth of the new churches there. What we do find from this chapter are the following: Paul was on Crete preaching the Gospel and starting churches, in numerous towns there were churches that were started, and in these same towns there was a leadership vacuum which is the reason Paul writes this letter to Titus. We do find in Acts 27 one reference to Paul on Crete while he was en route to Rome.[13] Was this when Paul began preaching the Gospel on Crete and churches were planted? We simply do not know. However, what we do know was that there were churches in numerous towns that needed elders to lead and oversee them.

I do not advocate that Paul was working from this concept of a multi-nucleated church, but there certainly are commonalities, especially when we look at Crete. Titus was charged to establish elders in the towns where churches were being birthed. I would surmise that in some capacity that they were all somehow inter-connected. Maybe it wasn't a formal

---

[13] Acts 27:7-8.

structure in the sense of the networks and denominations we have today, but perhaps they were at least connected through Titus as overall leader. We do not have the luxury of any more detail. Did these churches in various towns ever gather with one another? Did they go on mountain retreats together? Did they care for each others' needs as we find multiple times in Acts when churches financially supported other churches? Did they share their leaders? Did teachers rotate among the churches? How many different churches or gatherings were there in each town? We simply do not know. What only know that Titus was instructed to set up elders in each of the towns that had churches. Everything else becomes conjecture.

What this brief passage in Titus highlights is the fluidity of the early church. In some ways though we see a continuous pattern of leadership as found throughout Acts and in the Pauline epistles. Churches are established and leaders are chosen. In this case, Titus is to appoint these elders, while he himself oversees them. These leaders or elders are then empowered to lead the individual churches.

Without making too much of it, we find three layers or levels of leadership. Each location has an elder or elders leading the church, but then overarching multiple locations is someone like Titus giving leadership and direction to each of these church elders. And Paul is overseeing Titus. The leadership structure of the multi-nucleated church is now coming into focus. Let me begin piecing things together for how I envision the multi-nucleated church to work.

Putting the Pieces Together

This brief trek into three separate passages of the early church in the New Testament provides the beginnings of a template, or at least a conceptual framework, of a multi-nucleated church. I doubt I need to readdress my position, however I have no intention of making definitive or tight-fisted statements about how leadership is to be done in the church today. I contend that a lot of the how is fluid and adaptable based upon cultural dynamics. But I have some opinions as to *who* the leaders ought to be and *what* this leadership looks like. If we take Scripture at face value[14] the *who* are godly men (elders) and the *what* is that these men are to be full of integrity, dignity, and blameless. To take a short detour, as alluded to earlier, I believe that being a pastor or shepherd is a gifting more than a title or position (although they can be one and the same). Also, I do not believe that the Holy Spirit gives certain gifts based upon gender. However, the elders overseeing pastors and the overall church are to be godly men.

---

[14] I am mindful of the need to wade through Scripture with humility as we seek to discern between what was and is cultural and what was and is a universal principle that transcends all times and cultures.

What we find in the early church, and it's my contention that this applies to the multi-nucleated church, is that there was both a shared leadership as well as shared resources. The strength of this concept is that as one church in multiple locations there can be a sharing of resources from finances to talent and leadership. Think of the multi-nucleated church as a church co-op. This gets to the heart of what we find in the church birthed at Pentecost. "And all who believed were together and had all things in common. And they were selling their possessions and belongings and distributing the proceeds to all, as any had need."[15] The framework for a multi-nucleated church also carries with it some of the DNA that we find in the early church, particularly the example that we looked at on the island of Crete. Although it is one church, or one church network, there are multiple nuclei with multiple heads or leaders. Each site or gathering would have at least one elder and even more depending on the size of the church. This is where I part ways with the exclusively house church model. I am not opposed to churches that meet in homes, but the focus needs to be on the planting of churches across the community, whether in homes, coffee shops, schools, public houses, community centers, and so on. The bottom line is the planting of churches with context and leadership determining how they are planted and organized. The consistent element throughout is both a shared leadership and a shared DNA.

---

[15] Acts 2:44-45.

Chapter 7

While each gathering, site, or church has one or more elders in charge, collectively these elders form the overall leadership of the multi-nucleated church. In other words, leaders lead their local congregation and then they join with the larger network of other leaders to give direction to the network. And just as with Paul and Titus on Crete, there are overseers (bishops?) who give leadership to the network of elders. This is nothing new. There have been and continue to be variations of this concept of doing church. What may differ is that one church may exist in multiple locations as opposed to several churches making up a network or a denomination. This is a multi-nucleated ecclesiology.

In the context of each of the local gatherings in a variety of urban hubs or city centers, it is my contention that the best leadership structures find their fulfillment in the five-fold giftings as found in Ephesians 4:11-12. "And he gave the apostles, the prophets, the evangelists, the shepherds and teachers, to equip the saints for the work of ministry, for building up the body of Christ." These churches are led by a combination of those empowered by the Spirit to serve as an apostle, prophet, evangelist, pastor, and teacher. In practical terms, some of these leaders would also double as elders, but not necessarily in every case. People carry out their roles based upon giftedness.

There is much more I could say, but I will leave it there for the purposes of this book. It becomes problematic to make certain definitive statements when developing a theoretical framework. In time, it will get easier as these concepts becomes a reality in various settings and a lot of the issues and questions have been hammered out on the fly and in context. My intent here was to simply provide an overall example of how this would or could look. Leadership needs to be simple and nimble as the church expands along transportation lines.

Afterword

Moving Toward a Multi-Nucleated Church

"The inequities of heavily car dependent cities for the elderly, the young, and the poor, will be reduced by greater walkability and transit access; the social issues such as noise, neighborhood severance, road rage, and loss of public safety will be reduced; the economic costs from loss of productive agricultural land to sprawl and bitumen, the costs of accidents, pollution, and congestion, all will be reduced."[1] Throughout this book I have worked towards developing a multi-nucleated ecclesiology predicated upon the built environment and transportation infrastructure of polycentric cities as informed by Scripture. My desire was not to be novel or new, but rather as a missiologist to learn how to adapt around urban form.

Simply put, we need to stop creating churches in our minds that are void of culture and context. It is the context of

---

[1] Newman, et al., *Resilient Cities*, 10.

the city which is influential. Churches, while seeking to engage culture, often overlook the transportation technologies that also play a major shaping role in cities. This book has been an attempt to broach this subject and move the conversation forward.

A topic like this often opens the doors for even more questions and thoughtful reasoning. As the quotation at the beginning of this final section points out, the social issues surrounding transportation technologies is a good crossroads for the church to engage in. Yet this engagement may not even be pastor- or elder-led. In other words, this does not fall along conventional lines. In places like outer SE or outer NE Portland where many lower-income people and minorities are moving to, there is often an absence of good public transportation. Since these communities were built during the era of the automobile they did not develop the density needed to support such things as light-rail, streetcars, or a more robust bus system (or bicycle network). This is where the church can play a role in being a voice for those who may not have a voice, by helping to retrofit urbia (or suburbia) to provide adequate transportation infrastructure for its lower-income and marginalized residents. Maybe it is precisely at this intersection in culture and public policy where the church needs to be more engaged.

A multi-nucleated church is not simply about taking at face value what the city offers in terms of infrastructure and

Afterword

transportation technologies. It also seeks to play a role in shaping and influencing the future. A church planting movement should be about redeeming both urban people and urban places. My hope is that during the course of this short book you have been stretched and challenged anew in the way you look at your city and church planting. In that regard, this book serves simply as a primer for further theological reflection and ultimately action towards renewing our cities through church planting.

The Multi-Nucleated Church

Bibliography

Aronowitz, Nona. "Most Americans Want a Walkable Neighborhood, Not a Big House." *GOOD*, February 7, 2012. Online: http://www.good.is/post/most-americans-want-a-walkable-neighborhood-not-a-big-house.

Bakke, Ray. *A Theology as Big as the City.* Downers Grove: InterVarsity, 1997.

Bartholomew, Craig. *Where Mortals Dwell: A Christian View of Place for Today.* Grand Rapids: Baker Academic, 2011.

Benesh, Sean. *Metrospiritual: The Geography of Church Planting.* Eugene: Resource, 2011.

———. *View From the Urban Loft: Developing a Theological Framework for Understanding the City.* Eugene: Resource, 2011.

Brugmann, Jeb. *Welcome to the Urban Revolution: How Cities are Changing the World.* Toronto: Viking Canada, 2009.

Carr, Austin. "Innovative Mayor Sam Adams Builds a Cleaner Portland." *Fast Company,* June 17, 2010. Online: http://www.fastcompany.com/article/sam-adams-mayor-of-portland.

City of North Vancouver. "Livable Region Strategic Plan." *The City of North Vancouver*. Online: http://www.cnv.org/server.aspx?c=3&i=489.

———. "Lower Lonsdale," *The City of North Vancouver*. Online: http://www.cnv.org/server.aspx?c=2&i=91.

City of Portland Bureau of Planning and Sustainability. "Status Report: Twenty-minute Neighborhoods," *Portland Plan* (2009).

Cizek, Caterina. "One Millionth Tower," *National Film Board of Canada.* Online: http://highrise.nfb.ca/onemillionthtower/1mt_webgl.php.

Conn, Harvie and Manuel Ortiz. *Urban Ministry: The Kingdom, the City, and the People of God.* Downers Grove: IVP Academic, 2001.

Dear, Michael. *From Chicago to L.A.: Making Sense of Urban Theory.* Thousand Oaks: Sage, 2002.

Florida, Richard. *Who's Your City? How the Creative Economy is Making Where to Live the Most Important Decision in Your Life.* New York: Basic, 2008.

Garrison, David. *Church Planting Movements.* Richmond: IMB, 2000.

Gibson, K. "Bleeding Albina: A History of Community Disinvestment, 1940-2000." *Transforming Anthropology* 15:1 (2007): 3-25.

Glaeser, Edward. *Triumph of the City: How Our Greatest Invention Makes Us Richer, Smarter, Greener, Healthier, and Happier.* New York: Penguin, 2011.

Glaeser, E., and J. Gottlieb. "The Wealth of Cities: Agglomeration Economics and Spatial Equilibrium in the United States." *Journal of Economic Literature* 47 (2009): 983-1028.

Greenstone, M., et al. "Identifying Agglomeration Spillovers: Evidence From Winners and Losers of Large Plant Openings." *Journal of Political Economy* 118 (2010): 536-598.

Heying, Charles. *Brew to Bikes: Portland's Artisan Economy.* Portland: Ooligan, 2010.

Hiller, Harry. *Urban Canada.* New York: Oxford University Press, 2009.

Hirsch, Alan. *The Forgotten Ways: Reactivating the Missional Church*. Grand Rapids: Brazos, 2009.

Bibliography

Hirsch, Alan, and Tim Catchim. *The Permanent Revolution: Apostolic Imagination and Practice for the 21st Century Church*. San Francisco: Jossey-Bass, 2012.

Portland State University Senior Capstone and Multnomah County Library, "Hollywood Neighborhood History." *Historical Highlights of Hollywood*. Online: http://hollywood.pdx.edu/index.html.

Hughes, Wes. "PDX20: Church Planting in '20-Minute Communities" (brochure for church planter recruitment, Portland, Oregon).

Jacobsen, Eric. *Sidewalks in the Kingdom: New Urbanism and the Christian Faith*. Grand Rapids: Brazos, 2003.

Kolenko, Sean. "A Fisher of Men—The Life of a Church Planter," *North Shore Outlook*, April 6, 2011. Online: http://www.northshoreoutlook.com/news/119355179.html.

Levinson, David, and Kevin Krizek, *Planning for Place and Plexus: Metropolitan Land Use and Transport*. New York: Routledge, 2008.

Mapes, Jeff. *Pedaling Revolution: How Cyclists are Changing American Cities*. Corvallis: Oregon State University Press, 2009.

McAlpine, William. *Sacred Space for the Missional Church: Engaging Culture Through the Built Environment*. Eugene: Wipf and Stock, 2011.

Metro Vancouver. "Livable Centres," *Metro Vancouver*. Online: http://www.metrovancouver.org/planning/development/livablecentres/Pages/default.aspx.

Newman, Peter, et al, *Resilient Cities: Responding to Peak Oil and Climate Change*. Washington: Island Press, 2009.

Ng, Edward, *Designing High-Density Cities: For Social and Environmental Sustainability*. London: Earthscan, 2010.

Ott, Craig, and Gene Wilson. *Global Church Planting: Biblical Principles and Best Practices for Multiplication*. Grand Rapids: Baker Academic, 2011.

Patrick, Darrin, and Matt Carter, *For the City: Proclaiming and Living Out the Gospel*. Grand Rapids: Zondervan, 2010.

Phillips, E. Barbara, *City Lights: Urban-Suburban Life in the Global* Society. New York: Oxford University Press, 2010.

Shrout, Rick. *Street Crossers: Conversations with Simple Church Planters and Stories of Those Who Send Them.* Eugene: Wipf and Stock, 2011.

Smith, Duncan. "Polycentric Cities and Sustainable Development" (one page flyer).

Stetzer, Ed, and Warren Bird. *Viral Churches: Helping Church Planers Become Movement Makers.* San Francisco: Jossey-Bass, 2010.

Swanson, Eric, and Sam Williams. *To Transform a City: Whole Church, Whole Gospel, Whole City.* Grand Rapids: Zondervan, 2010.

UN-HABITAT. *Global Report on Human Settlement 2009: Planning Sustainable* Cities. London: Earthscan, 2009.

Urban Dictionary LLC. "Hipster." *Urban Dictionary*. Online: http://www.urbandictionary.com/define.php?term=hipster.

White, Richard. "Draft Metro Vancouver Regional Growth Strategy." (2009).

Wikimedia Foundation, Inc. "Los Angeles School." *Wikipedia*. Online: http://en.wikipedia.org/wiki/Los_Angeles_School.

About Urban Loft Publishers

Urban Loft Publishers focuses on ideas, topics, themes, and conversations about all things urban. Renewing the city is the central theme and focus of what we publish. It is our intention to blend urban ministry, theology, urban planning, architecture, urbanism, stories, and the social sciences, as ways to drive the conversation. While we lean towards scholarly and academic works, we explore the fun and lighter sides of cities as well. We publish a wide variety of urban perspectives, from books by the experts *about* the city to personal stories and personal accounts of urbanites who *live* in the city.

www.theurbanloft.org

About the Author

Coffee and bicycles define Sean's urban existence who believes the best way for exploring cities is on the seat of a bicycle as well as hanging out in third wave coffee shops. Sean is an urban missiologist who works in a creative partnership between TEAM as the Developer of Urban Strategy and Training and the Upstream Collective leading the PDX Loft.

www.seanbenesh.com

Books in the Metrospiritual Book Series

The Bikeable Church: A Bicyclist's Guide to Church Planting
(2012)

Blueprints for a Just City: The Role of the Church in Urban Planning and Shaping the City's Built Environment
(coming in 2015)

Made in the USA
Lexington, KY
06 December 2016